Brand
Busters

Practical Books for Smart Marketers from PMP

Marketing, Market Research

The 4Cs of Truth in Communication:
  How to Identify, Discuss, Evaluate and Present Stand-out, Effective Communication
Consumer Insights 2.0:
  How Smart Companies Apply Customer Knowledge to the Bottom Line
Dominators, Cynics, and Wallflowers:
  Practical Strategies for Moderating Meaningful Focus Groups
Moderating to the Max!
  A Full-Tilt Guide to Creative, Insightful Focus Groups and Depth Interviews
Outsmart the MBA Clones
  The Alternative Guide to Competitive Strategy, Marketing, and Branding
The Mirrored Window: *Focus Groups from a Moderator's Point of View*
Religion in a Free Market: *Religious and Non-Religious Americans—*
  Who, What, Why, Where
Why People Buy Things They Don't Need

Mature Market/ Baby Boomers

Advertising to Baby Boomers
After Fifty: *How the Baby Boom Will Redefine the Mature Market*
After Sixty: *Marketing to Baby Boomers Reaching Their Big Transition Years*
Baby Boomers and Their Parents:
  Surprising Findings about Their Lifestyles, Mindsets, and Well-Being
Marketing to Leading-Edge Baby Boomers
The Boomer Heartbeat:
  Capturing the Heartbeat of the Baby Boomers Now and in the Future

Multicultural

Beyond Bodegas: *Developing a Retail Relationship with Hispanic Customers*
Hispanic Marketing Grows Up: *Exploring Perceptions and Facing Realities*
Hispanic Customers for Life: *A Fresh Look at Acculturation*
Latinization: *How Latino Culture Is Transforming the U.S.*
Marketing to American Latinos: *A Guide to the In-Culture Approach, Part I & II*

Marketing to American Latinos: A Guide to the In-Culture Approach, Part II

The Whole Enchilada: *Hispanic Marketing 101*
What's Black About It?
  Insights to Increase Your Share of a Changing African-American Market

Youth Markets

The Kids Market: *Myths & Realities*
Marketing to the New Super Consumer: Mom & Kid
The Great Tween Buying Machine: *Marketing to Today's Tweens*

Marketing Management

A Clear Eye for Branding: *Straight Talk on Today's Most Powerful Business Concept*
A Knight's Code of Business:
  How to Achieve Character and Competence in the Corporate World
Beyond the Mission Statement: *Why Cause-Based Communications Lead to True Success*
India Business: *Finding Opportunities in this Big Emerging Market*
Marketing Insights to Help Your Business Grow

Brand Busters

7 Common Mistakes Marketers Make

Lessons from the world of
technical and scientific products

Chris Wirthwein

Paramount Market Publishing, Inc.

Paramount Market Publishing, Inc.
950 Danby Road, Suite 136
Ithaca, NY 14850
www.paramountbooks.com
Telephone: 607-275-8100; 888-787-8100   Facsimile: 607-275-8101

Publisher: James Madden
Editorial Director: Doris Walsh

Cataloging in Publication Data available
ISBN 978-0-9801745-0-2

Contents

Acknowledgements

I COLLECT THINGS; ALWAYS HAVE. Truth is, I have trouble throwing stuff away—never know when you'll find a good use for something, right?

You hold in your hands one of my collections—a collection not of things, however, but of *ideas*. Think of this book as an assemblage of marketing concepts I've heard, witnessed, read, synthesized, and in many cases dreamed up, over the past few decades. Looking back, I can say I had a ball assembling it, and I figured it was about time I let others take a look at it. I hope you enjoy examining it, but more so, I hope there's something in here you can put to good use.

Beyond the ideas, though, I've collected something much more important and enduring and that is the relationships I have with others. And so to friends, family, colleagues, advisors and clients, without whom I would never have been able to start, much less complete this book, I say thank you. Specifically, my sincere gratitude goes out to:

Noel and Jo Callahan, from whom I learned about business, about marketing, and about making big dreams come true. Jo and Noel, you always believed in me. Whatever I've achieved in business, I owe in great measure to you.

Steve Hilger, who brings boldness, a never-say-die attitude and true marketing creativity into all that he does. How fortunate I've been to be able to work alongside you. Folks, if working with Steve doesn't get you enthused about marketing, you simply don't have it in you to be enthused. Thanks for the many years of trust and inspiration.

Ken Honeywell, dear friend and writing partner in this adventure. You believed in the idea of this book and you didn't quit believing until we got it done. Thanks, Ken—we did it!

Joe Bannon, client, friend, and sage counselor for most of my career. Joe, what I've learned from you about global marketing, advertising, branding, dealing with people and how to be a good agency could fill a book—and lots of it has!

Jim DeCoursey, who taught me the value of precision and discipline in marketing—and the value of taking an afternoon every once in a while to philosophize about the world. Live it up, Jim. The world is a better place with you in it.

Dr. Greg Sipes, philosopher, author, true friend, and kindred soul. You've helped me see differently and to understand that what you are and how you see makes all the difference. My world's a better place because of you, Greg.

Mark Duffin who has been at my side through thick and thin longer than just about anyone. Nobody has been a better collaborator, a better organizer, or a better finisher than you. Nobody. Who knows where 5MetaCom would be without you? (I do. It wouldn't be nearly as far along.)

Jerry Hoover, high school teacher and mentor who taught me the true meaning of the word excellence. Mr. Hoover, you not only set high standards, you inspired us to achieve them. (And you taught us how.) Your positive impact on the world lives on.

My Mom and Dad. Maybe I wasn't the best kid in the world, but you never let on. Without being too sappy, I can say no kid ever had it better growing up. You let us do just about anything we wanted to do, and lo and behold, now one of your kids has even written a book! It's no wonder.

My wife Sally, son Alex, and daughter Grace. Sure business is important, but you're the real deal. What am I without you?

Nothing much. Thanks for letting me be something really, really important—a husband and a father.

The many, many professional, talented and just plain good people who have worked at my company, 5MetaCom, over the years. I've always felt sheepish accepting praise for what we've accomplished for our clients for I know the bulk of the hard work and creativity behind the results has come from you. I'm fortunate to stand on the shoulders of giants.

To every client of 5MetaCom, past, present and future. Without you, there is no 5MetaCom (and no book). And we like it that way. The free enterprise system works wonders, for it allows us to serve at your pleasure. That means you have to be pleased—and I wouldn't have it any other way.

And finally, the four years of writing are over. So to all who read this book . . . enjoy!

CHRIS WIRTHWEIN
NOVEMBER 2007

Preface

Every marketer of every kind of product or service will benefit from the lessons contained in this book.

A startling claim? Yes, because, the Brand Busters presented themselves to me within the highly focused field of technical and scientific product marketing, an arena not every marketer works in.

Over more than decades I've been navigating these fairly complex waters, helping my clients market sophisticated products to hyper-educated, hyper-savvy, hyper-critical audiences: physicians, PhDs, engineers, commercial real estate owners, laboratory equipment buyers, food producers and manufacturers, veterinarians, IT directors, hospital administrators, drug development scientists—the list goes on and on. I've created marketing strategies, communications campaigns, and tactical marketing tools for dozens upon dozens of products from some of the world's most respected marketers and brands: Bristol-Myers, Firestone, Roche Diagnostics, Black & Decker, Land O' Lakes, Eli Lilly and Company, Honeywell, Dow AgroSciences, as well as scores of lesser known, yet highly successful companies.

During the process of writing the book you now hold in your hands, I had a clear picture of "you"—the reader—in mind. I imagined "you" to be a marketing director or an advertising or communications manager at a company brimming with technical and scientific products to sell—new wonder chemistries, technological breakthroughs, engineering marvels—rocket science stuff, perhaps.

As a bit of personal background, you should know that I didn't always work in this highly specialized market. Early in my career I worked for a time with general consumer products, mainly retailing, apartment housing, and entertainment. I had some fun and got my feet wet with TV, radio, newspaper, direct mail, couponing, and outdoor advertising. Yet, I found myself being drawn to a much different group of clients, those whose marketing proved to me to be more interesting and more demanding. I became hooked on the world of technical and scientific products. To me, the marketing problems here seemed more challenging, and more rewarding to solve. The audiences seemed more critical and more difficult to sway—and so the victory in winning them over tasted that much sweeter.

As I progressed in my career, I discovered the importance of strategy. I realized it took more than a witty phrase or shocking visual to earn a customer's business. And I learned how to communicate clearly and succinctly and with the buyers' wants always front and center. Most of all, I learned how to think more critically when evaluating business trends, market data, advertising plans, creative approaches, customer feedback, client input, and the like. After a couple of decades in the vortex of this demanding arena, I realized it was time to speak up about what I'd learned. So I wrote this book for my colleagues, friends, and competitors who, like I, face the daily challenge of marketing technical and scientific products.

And yet, as I finished reading my work, I realized just how much I have learned from others *outside* my specific area of marketing. I am reminded of great marketing minds I learned from along the way. Authors, teachers, practitioners from entirely different fields of marketing, communications, and advertising than the one I know. From David Ogilvy, Trout and Ries, Claude Hopkins, John Caples, and many others I learned marketing and strategy lessons from the world of consumer packaged goods, mail order advertising, autos, airlines, and myriad other industries. Those lessons absolutely have helped me and my clients market their technical and scientific products.

Don't get me wrong; I certainly didn't pick up any lessons I could simply cut and paste into a ready made solution. Instead, I learned marketing principles—foundational concepts—that I could apply to many different and varied situations beyond their original scope.

I guarantee this same thing has happened to you and me throughout our years of formal schooling. Need proof? I'll give you some examples.

In my college Shakespeare class I learned the power of words, how words and *words alone* can make you and I laugh . . . or cry. I use these Shakespearean principles today to help my clients make compelling emotional appeals to their customers and prospects. In high school chemistry I learned how to determine the effect of a certain action by changing just a single variable in an experiment. I've used that knowledge throughout my career when attempting to determine the effect of a specific promotional activity on sales. So The Bard and Alexander Fleming taught me marketing? Absolutely.

And that's why I'm convinced that no matter what type of marketing you do—whether it's menswear or molecular markers—you'll discover principles in this book that you can apply to your specific situation.

To those who work in the same field as your author: welcome colleague. And to those who don't, I say, jump on in. The water's fine. You're bound to find a few new ideas swimming around in this fascinating microcosm we call technical and scientific marketing. Let's get started.

Introduction

I just wanted to buy a telescope.

Let me explain: I was born in the midst of the Space Age. I grew up in the 1960s and 1970s. Astronauts were my heroes. I was sure that one day, I too would be an astronaut, piloting missions to Mars and the outer planets, maybe even reaching beyond the limits of our solar system and journeying to the nearest star. Even if this dream didn't come true, I could still be an astronomer, discovering stars, searching for alien life forms, and, most of all, gazing into the night sky through a great, big telescope. Man... that was going to be cool.

Of course, life didn't turn out that way. My love of astronomy took a back seat to baseball, then girls, then more creative pursuits. I discovered I had a talent for writing and a mind for marketing, and that I actually enjoyed business. I went into advertising and eventually owned my own ad agency that specializes in marketing for technical and scientific products—that is, products in which science and engineering are integral to marketing.

In other words, although I was doing something very different from astronomy, science—as it applies to advertising and marketing—has been part of my life for a long time. Not too long ago, it occurred to me that it was finally time to indulge my childhood fantasy and start to explore the universe again. As I said, I wanted to buy a telescope.

I began where lots of people begin these days: on the Internet.

Surely, there were plenty of telescope companies with websites. Surely, any one of them would be happy to sell me the telescope that I had the means and the motivation to buy. I had no intention of pussyfooting around or haggling over nickels and dimes. I was going to be an easy sell. Sure, I wanted to make a smart decision, but mostly I wanted to see the stars and planets.

But did anyone make it easy for me to buy?

No. Everyone talked over my head. On every website I visited, the copy seemed to have been written not for humans but for some race of unemotional alien beings. I was promised diffraction-limited Schmidt-Newtonians, achromatic refraction, and German-type equatorial mounting. I was enticed with enhanced aluminum coatings and large aperture Dobsonians and removable truss systems.

Thank goodness for *Sky and Telescope* magazine. I went to its website and found articles written in plain English that offered me excellent advice about telescopes that might be right for me; in fact, I gladly paid to download these articles from their archive. They spoke to me as an intelligent and interested novice, telling me what equipment I needed to see the stars and the planets—which is all I really wanted to do.

Once I'd read up on telescopes in *Sky and Telescope,* I went back to the web. I discovered that you don't buy telescopes from manufacturers; you buy from a dealer. You would think the dealers' websites would be customer friendly; after all, these were the folks who were actually dealing with the public.

Wrong. If anything, they were more muddled and confusing than the manufacturers' sites. I started to get discouraged all over again. Finally, I called one of the dealers and talked with a salesperson who listened to me and helped me get the telescope I wanted.

What's that Sizzling Sound?

Most marketers can spot the big mistake the telescope companies made. It was a classic example of companies selling the features of their products rather than the benefits to consumers: "selling the steak instead of the sizzle," to paraphrase an old advertising chest-nut. McDonald's for example, is not really in the fast food business; they're in the family entertainment business. They just happen to sell hamburgers. The features may be two all-beef patties, special sauce, and all the rest, but the benefit is happy kids. Watch a couple of McDonald's television spots and see if you don't agree.

However, it's one thing to identify a problem and quite another to understand it. And when it comes to marketing for technical and scientific products, it's a problem that grows out of ideas that are deeply wired into the brains of the marketers. Believe it or not, **they think we care about that stuff.**

Undoubtedly, there are people who understand diffraction-limited Schmidt-Newtonians and all that; in fact, now that I'm a telescope owner, I'm one of them. Undoubtedly, the telescope manufacturers sell their products to those people.

The question is, which is larger? The group of people who under-stand the technical design of telescopes, or the group that just wants to look at the stars? And if it's possible to reach a larger group with a persuasive message, wouldn't you want to do that?

And here's the real question: wouldn't your smaller, telescope-loving audience also respond better if you talked to them like real people instead of technogeeks?

Telescope Marketing Through the Microscope

I would suggest that you can learn a number of lessons from my experience with telescope manufacturers.

The marketers gave away all their power to journalists. Nothing against journalists—they have a job to do and, in this case, they did it very well. I might have gone to *Sky and Telescope* looking for information, anyway; I generally don't make big purchases without at least some minimal due diligence. The point is, I *had* to go to the journalists. The marketers weren't telling me anything I could understand. They blew a great opportunity to make a sale—or at least a great impression.

I didn't need a lot of information. Nor did I *want* a lot of information. I wanted a little information. I wanted to know how much telescope I could buy for a couple of thousand dollars, and whether that was enough—or maybe too much—to get me the stargazing power I wanted. Could I get up-close and personal with Saturn? That was all I wanted to know.

I wanted. Note the most important words in the last paragraph: *I wanted.* I could have lived the rest of my life without a telescope, and when it came to features, I had no idea what I needed. I was totally driven by my desires.

The marketers made the salespeople work too hard. Thank goodness I ran into a salesperson who knew his stuff. And thank goodness I'd read up on telescopes before I called. Salespeople have a difficult and important enough job to do without having to do your marketing job as well. I should be far enough along in my buying decision when I talk to a salesperson that I can be pointed in the right direction to get the product I want.

If you're shaking your head at this point, pitying the poor telescope manufacturers and marketers who did such a questionable job of helping me buy a telescope, now might be a good time to stop. Because if you're marketing a technical or scientific product, you're probably making—or have made—the same mistakes. And chances are good that your product has a technical or scientific wrinkle to it, even if you don't realize it.

Are You a Technical Marketer?

You might think my story about trying to buy a telescope is an isolated incident. You might think it's pretty specialized; after all, most people *don't* buy telescopes. But let me ask you this:

How many automobile ads have you seen that try to impress you with valves and liters and horsepower and all sorts of bells and whistles?

What's the clock speed of the motherboard in your computer? The resolution of your HD plasma TV?

What exactly is it about Omega-3 fatty acids that are supposed to be good for you? How does ibuprofen stop a headache?

The fact is, there is science involved in all sorts of purchases we make every day. Sometimes we understand it. Sometimes we don't. Sometimes the science is involved in our decisions and sometimes it isn't. But what is certainly clear is that we want the benefits of the products science has created. And sometimes the benefits are all the science we need to understand:

- "That car goes fast and makes me look cool."
- "This computer is easy to use."
- "The picture on this big screen looks terrific."
- "I feel like I have more energy when I take Omega-3."
- "I take ibuprofen and my headache goes away."

So let's agree on a definition of technical and scientific products: Technical and scientific products (or services) are those in which science or engineering plays a key role in marketing.

For our purposes, it doesn't matter whether science or engineering is involved in the manufacturing of your product. There's certainly a fair amount of science and engineering in creating the hamburgers you buy at McDonald's, but it generally doesn't find its way into their advertising.

On the other hand, if you're selling animal health products to the beef producers who raise the cattle for McDonald's hamburgers, that's technical/scientific marketing. If you're cold-forming steel parts or selling machines that create cold-formed steel parts, that's technical/scientific marketing.

In fact, when you stop and think about it, most manufacturers, healthcare companies, electronics companies, agribusinesses, trade advertisers, and consumer advertisers of all sorts are involved in technical marketing. And if you think your company may be involved, you're particularly prone to a whole host of common mistakes.

Common Mistakes on Parade

Here is where I let you in on the dirty little secret of this book: I'm well qualified to tell you about the dumb things marketers do to bust their brands, because I've done every one of them. Some of these mistakes I've made repeatedly. Early in my career, I unwittingly advised my clients to make them. Thankfully, because I work with nice people, I've kept my early clients in spite of my bad advice. We learned to be smarter together.

I tell you this because I want you to know that the subtitle of this book means exactly what it says: these are common mistakes *all* people involved with technical/scientific product marketing make. Including me. Including you.

Fortunately, you don't have to make them anymore. You can learn from my mistakes.

In Chapter 1, I'll talk about one of the fatal errors committed by the marketers I ran into when looking for a telescope: talking "needs" instead Of "wants." Most technical marketers believe that their customers make purchase decisions based on rational "needs," when nothing could be further from the truth. This condition leads marketers to lecture their customers as if they were unemotional robots instead of people. (I know what you're thinking: "You don't get it, Chris. My audience is different. They're highly educated. They're MDs/DVMs/PhDs/engineers/geeks." I hear you. Keep reading.) But even highly technical purchases are made because of people's emotional wants; in fact, only when you first engage people on an emotional level can you communicate the features that appeal to their rational side.

Chapter 2 addresses the biggest issue I had with telescope marketers: falling in love with your product instead of your customer. To the people who made them, I'm sure the diffraction-limited Schmidt-Newtonians seem wonderful—amazing, even. To me, those words got in the way of giving them the thousands of dollars I was willing to spend. This mistake is particularly insidious, because many technical/scientific marketers labor under the false assumption that their market is somehow different and that their customers are specialized nerds who prefer being talked to in obfuscatory language (er, that's "complicated words"). As a result, they fall prey to crowing about product features and forget their customers care about features only because of what they can *do*.

This goes hand-in-hand with the next brand buster: believing that marketing is a science or an art, the subject of Chapter 3. Although there are many scientific aspects to effective advertising, treating advertising wholly as a science leads to analysis paralysis and can end up stifling your marketing efforts. The flip side of this common mistake is just as common. Sure, there is artistry involved in the creation of great, effective advertising. But treating advertising solely as an art often leads to allowing a very small tail to wag a very large dog—with predictably (that is to say, scientifically) disastrous results.

In Chapter 4, we'll explore another double-edged mistake: trying to please everyone. This leads marketers in two equally misguided directions. On one hand, they may try to create plans that treat everyone the same and dilute their most powerful marketing messages. On the other hand, they may divide and subdivide their audience in a way that makes their efforts wildly, and needlessly, expensive.

The next common mistake can be another insidious one: forgetting that people forget. Advertising frequency is a great and powerful marketing tool. People buy what they prefer (want) and people prefer what they're aware of (I'll show you the science that backs it up). You can buy awareness and build preference, but only if you keep up your frequency. Market research reveals plenty about how often you need to talk to your audience to get them to remember and prefer your product. It's information that's just plain stupid to ignore—but most technical marketers do, anyway.

Chapter 6 is important for any marketer who faces aggressive competition. It's a mistake most marketers make at one time or another: believing your price is too high without proof. When faced with buyer resistance—perhaps as reported by salespeople—some marketers use price-cutting as their strategy of first resort, which often does nothing but damage your market and your brand while you reduce your profitability. Customers will usually pay more for the product they really want. Price-cutting is often a lazy and ultimately destructive short-term solution.

The common mistake in Chapter 7 is closely aligned with price-cutting: believing you can sell your product only on an economic basis. In study after study, in market after market—even those markets for what people define as "commodity" products—buyers usually place price in the middle of the pack on the list of purchase criteria. Many other factors are more important than cost savings or even ROI. Sometimes, the biggest factor in someone's buying decision is that they want to do business with people they like—people who they perceive understand and care about them.

Finally, in Chapter 8, I'll recap and tie together all the common mistakes with a few basic, universal principles that transcend any given mistake—and help you become a really good marketer in about a minute (really).

How Many Mistakes Did You Make Today?

Maybe you're not making all of these mistakes. Maybe some are affecting you more than others.

But there's another possibility: *maybe you're making these mistakes and you don't even know it.*

Trust me, it's not only possible, but likely. We all like to think we're just a little bit smarter than our competition. We also like to think the rules that apply to most marketing situations don't really apply to us. Any of these phrases sound familiar to you?

"My market is totally different from other markets."

"You can't talk to doctors, engineers/purchasers/fill-in-the-blank without a lot of technical language."

"We have to show a picture of our product in the ad."

"All our customers care about is price."

"We don't get any leads from advertising in that magazine, so it must be worthless."

"Our product does a great job of fulfilling our customers' unique needs."

"We ran an ad last month. Why should we run one this month?"

"Yes, the type is a little hard to read. But it looks a lot nicer this way."

"Nobody reads long copy anymore."

"In our market, it's all about ROI, and only about ROI."

Chances are you've said, heard, or believed at least one of these statements in the past month. And these statements just scratch the surface of the faulty ideas I'll debunk in the chapters ahead.

If one of the common mistakes described above rings particularly true for you, feel free to skip ahead to that chapter. Every day you keep making that mistake is another day you're compromising your marketing effectiveness.

However, I'd also encourage you to read up on all the mistakes. Remember, these are mistakes that all of us have made and continue to make—sometimes without our knowledge. These mistakes can be so subtle they show up again and again, and unless we keep them at the forefront of our thinking about marketing, we'll continue to make them. After all, one of the mistakes is forgetting that people forget. That includes me—and you.

All in all, I think it will be an entertaining and enlightening ride—one that's worth the effort. Leo Burnett, founder of the ad agency that still bears his name and has produced some of the most memorable consumer and retail campaigns in advertising history, once said, "Reach for the stars. You might not get one . . . but you probably won't come up with a handful of mud, either." Good advice—whether you're marketing package goods or hamburgers. Or telescopes.

Ready to get started? All you have to do is reach for the next page.

Brand Buster #1

Talking "Needs" Instead of "Wants"

THERE IS A CLASSIC MARKETING STORY about Samuel Johnson, usually known as "Dr. Johnson," the eighteenth century British lexicographer, author, and leading light of London literary society. As told by the late David Ogilvy in his classic 1983 book *Ogilvy on Advertising,*[1] Dr. Johnson once was responsible for auctioning off the contents of the Anchor Brewery. Dr. Johnson, ever the careful wordsmith and brilliant conversationalist, told his audience: "We are not here to sell boilers and vats, but the potentiality of growing rich beyond the dreams of avarice." (Avarice is a pretty uncommon word these days. It means "an excessive desire for riches.")

That is an offer pretty difficult to refuse. Certainly, you *need* boilers and vats to run a brewery. But what you really *want* is to be rich. More than 200 years ago, Dr. Johnson knew clearly what most—dare I say all—technical/scientific marketers fail, at one time or another, to understand: wants are more powerful than needs. Stated another way, when it comes to making purchase decisions for just about anything, emotion rules and reason takes a back seat.

So why do most technical marketers fill their selling messages with boilers and vats?

The Need for "Need"

Ask a hundred marketing people what is the most overused word in marketing today, and I'm willing to bet the most popular answer

1

is "quality." This makes some sense; "quality" has become one of those feel-good words that is all but devoid of meaning. Yet marketers, advertisers, and salespeople are constantly claiming that the difference between their product and their competitors' is that "our quality is higher." (We're going to talk about quality in the next chapter, so stay tuned.)

I would respectfully disagree. I think the most overused word in technical marketing is "need." From boardrooms to shop floors, production meetings to job interviews, everybody talks needs. You've heard the comments. The CEO: "We've got to deliver what the market *needs*." The sales manager: "This product truly meets the buyer's *needs*." The head of research and development: "We looked at what the market *needs*, and this new generation development is aimed directly at meeting those *needs*." (Just for fun, type *meet your needs* into your favorite search engine and see how many hits you get. Google gave me 111 million. I hope one of them isn't yours.)

But does the market really need anything? If your product is delivering what the market needs, how come you're not selling more? And just who exactly is judging what the market needs, anyway? "Need" is not only overused, it's also dangerous.

Yes, dangerous. Dangerous because it's thrown around haphazardly. Dangerous because it's so wrongheaded and it seems so innocuous. Dangerous not only because of what it is, but what it represents: marketers who are out of touch with how and why their customers buy.

You don't actually *need* very much in this life. You have physiological needs, of course: food, water, shelter, a certain degree of comfort. If you ever had a high school or college psychology class, you might remember Maslow's Hierarchy of Needs, in which the psychologist Abraham Maslow created a "needs pyramid." Essentially, the idea is that you have to satisfy your most basic needs before ascending to the next level. If you aren't too tired or hungry, have plenty of air to breathe, and have your sexual urges more or less fulfilled (physiological needs), you can worry about safety needs: the security of home, family, and religion. Love needs came next, followed by esteem needs, and on up to self-actualization needs, or the need to realize your full potential.[2]

Right away, you'll notice two things about this list. First, most of Maslow's "needs" are needs only in the loosest sense of the word. You might need oxygen. But love is less of a need and more of a desire, which, actually, puts it more in the realm of wants. In any case, whether or not you agree with Maslow's arrangement of certain needs, (or whatever you want to call them), he was right to create a hierarchy. You certainly aren't thinking about realizing your fullest potential if you're cold and hungry.

The second thing you'll notice is that there is nothing on Maslow's list about press brakes or chromium picolinate. Nothing about disc drives or fertilizer. Nothing about televisions or tele-scopes.

That's because people don't buy what they *need*. People buy what they *want*.

Even at the most basic levels of Maslow's hierarchy, we buy what we want. Maslow was probably a fine psychologist, but as a marketer, he left something to be desired. He seems to assume we have little or no choice, and while this was true to a much greater degree in earlier times, it is usually not the case in our modern consumer culture. I need to eat, and if bread and water are the only options available to me, I'll eat them. But in most cases I choose what I want, and I don't want "food," I want hamburgers and iced tea. So that's what I buy. You can make this case right down the line: we need shelter from the elements, and although a tent would do, most of us want something more substantial. Unwashed jeans make adequate covers for our bodies, but I don't want to look like that. Business casual looks nicer—and I want to look nice.

You get the idea. Marketing is about choice. Which means it's about *wants*, not needs.

Emotion Is No Laughing Matter

So why do technical/scientific marketers think they're exempt from appealing to their customers' emotions? I think it's because emotions are . . . well, emotional.

As a culture, we have long been of the opinion that emotion is inferior to reason. Our nation's Founding Fathers crafted a constitution based on reasonable arguments, right? The West was won by grit and determination and better ways of doing things, and there weren't many sensitive types (artists, sculptors, musicians) around to stand in the way of progress. Sensitive men had their brief moments in the sun during the 1960s and 1970s, but a look at box office receipts showed that, even then, we mostly preferred (wanted) John Wayne and Clint Eastwood and Arnold Schwarzenegger, who exhibit manly emotions like anger.

Are you beginning to see a pattern here? Emotion is feminine, and feminine is weak-willed and certainly not businesslike.

This is, of course, hogwash—on a lot of different levels. But we can save the discussion of gender roles for another day (and another book). What's crucial to this particular argument is that technical/scientific marketing, especially, is perceived to be an overwhelmingly logical, factual, and what might be considered *masculine* discipline, in terms of both the audience technical/scientific marketers want to reach and the appropriate approach to that audience.

So the logical (masculine) approach seems to make sense. But, when it comes to selling, *emotion—not logic—is primary.* Period. Doesn't matter who you're selling to: men or women, physicists or psychics, engineers, or English teachers. People buy what they want; yet, technical/scientific marketers are rarely taught to focus on wants. They get schooled in needs-based marketing, and it's an approach that's simplistic and ultimately not as effective as wants-based marketing. That's because, ultimately, needs speak to features, while wants speak to benefits.

A quick example: Let's say Mark is in charge of his company's information technology department. He's had some trouble with hard drives on the company's servers; they've been unreliable, and others in the company have been complaining about losing data when the drives fail, which, in turn, leads to the problems of employees having poor access to the data they need to do their jobs.

What he *needs* is more reliable data storage.

But what he *wants* is for the employees to get off his back and stop complaining about the poor performance of the equipment he's supposed to be taking care of.

Which do *you* think is a more compelling message: "Higher capacity, hot-swappable data storage," or "Now you can get the employees off your back"?

I've made my point, perhaps a bit crudely. But it's the latter that Mark wants, right? Which is funny, because most technical marketers go out to meet their prospects with messages a lot closer to the former.

Moving Beyond Benefits

If you have spent much time in or around marketing circles, you've probably come up against the features-advantages-benefits continuum, which is the classic way of looking at product attributes and turning them into marketing messages. While this continuum begins to get at the right way to reach consumers for your product or service, I submit that it doesn't go far enough.

First, some definitions. To put it as simply as possible, features are attributes inherent in the product (size, weight, color, performance metrics, etc.); advantages are the meaningful things customers get out of those features; and benefits are the results of those advantages. For example, powerful sucking action is a feature of a vacuum cleaner. The advantage is that it cleans up more dog hair in less time. The benefit is that you have a cleaner home, with no more dog hair flying around.

Many technical/scientific marketing efforts start and end with features, which fits right in with the mistake of focusing on "things the market needs." Pick up any trade magazine in your industry, and I guarantee you'll find dozens of ads touting features in their headlines: cutting width, tolerances, formulation specs, ISO designations, horsepower per cc, cellular concentration levels, and on and on. It's difficult to move past features when you think your customers really need them. And again, needs relate to features.

But the cult of feature-advantage-benefit is so strong that most technical marketers *do* move to advantages—and stop. Advantages are the primary source of headlines in technical advertising; translating the above features into advantages might yield:

"Now cut larger workpieces than ever before."

"Take care of two problems with one herbicide."

"Tighter tolerances deliver less bleed-through."

"ISO 9001 certification means the quality is built in."

"The powerful machine that takes up less room in your lab."

"Smaller, yet more powerful."

"Faster out of the bloodstream and into the tissue."

Now, these are generic and bad headlines, made up in about a minute each. But they're remarkably similar to the majority of headlines you'll find in ads for technical products. Several of them border on being provocative; if I've had trouble cutting large workpieces, I might be interested in this advantage. If you understand my two toughest problems and can treat them with the same herbicide, I might be willing to read on.

The problem is, advantages still appeal to the intellectual side of the marketing equation. There is nothing emotional about larger workpieces; it is something I might recognize as advantageous to me, but it's not something that fills me with desire.

Talking about needs is also condescending. It says, "Never mind what you want. We're the experts here, and we know what's best for you." Do you like being lectured like that?

The other problem—at least as concerns the old feature-advantage-benefit model—is that marketers frequently confuse advantages with benefits. That's why it's so common for them to stop here; less bleed-through *seems* like a benefit. Taking care of two problems with one herbicide *seems* like a benefit.

So what are the benefits? Try these on for size: Put an end to lab tech turnover. Farm more acres with your existing labor and equipment. No overnight stay for your dog at the veterinary clinic.

Benefits start to address what people want—and wants speak to emotion. They get at the emotional issues involved in marketing your technical product or service; in fact, they start to get at the emotions so well that most technical marketers are reluctant to use benefits, regardless of the lip service they pay to them. That's why they often stop with advantages: they can't bring themselves to actually take that big step to the right side of the brain and talk about what people want.

And when they do, they often saddle themselves with the same sort of feature-advantages baggage their competitors drag around. The result is the creation of marketing messages that are far less compelling than they could or should be—and again, I believe it's because we have such a difficult time getting "needs" out of our heads. Even our "benefits" are driven by needs, which is so often why they default to financial considerations. Take any of the above examples, and you can spin them into dollar savings, higher productivity, profitability, and so forth. If it has to do with money, it must be a benefit.

I respectfully disagree. In Chapter 7, I talk about marketers who think they have to position their products mainly for some sort of economic benefit, and why that's a big mistake. Let's table that discussion for now, though, and look at what I think is a far better alternative to needs-based marketing.

A New Model: Wants-Based Marketing

Wants-based marketing moves past the entire needs-based feature-advantage-benefit continuum into something entirely new. If features are what I need, advantages are why I need them, and benefits are what the features do for me, *wants are what I care enough about to take action.* They are benefits imbued with an emotional charge.

Consumer and package good marketers have long been masters

of cutting through the feature-advantage-benefit morass to get to what we really want. We don't really want a beer that tastes delicious: we want to impress the woman at the table in the corner. We don't care how many seconds it takes to go from zero to sixty mph: we want people's jaws to drop when they see us drive past. Toothpaste isn't really about oral hygiene: it's about personal vanity. Dell understands that most computer buyers aren't really looking for gigahertz and clock speed and video cards. They're looking for simplicity and reliability.

Of course, a lot of technical/scientific marketing is aimed at a business or professional audience. To take the argument into the realm of technical marketing, the man (because it was certainly a man) who first thought to pose bikini-clad women next to shop tools on their calendars was a wants-based (albeit Neanderthal) marketer. He knew that mechanics wanted pictures of beautiful women more than they wanted utility or productivity.

Drivers of new car purchases

A 2005 study of new car purchases shows *want* or *desire* was the biggest motivator in purchase decisions.

I'm certainly not condoning this type of drivel in marketing—it's not only simplistic, it's also ugly and small minded. What I'm saying is that you must get to your customers' deep-seated wants and desires to move them to buy your technical product or service—just as the consumer goods marketers have done so well.

You might wonder if there are data to support the idea that wants are more compelling than needs. Wonder no longer: a research brief published by the Center for Media Research[3] showed the number one reason consumers buy a new car is "because I want one." A full 36 percent of respondents to a Vertis "Customer Focus" survey cited "want" as the winner. "Need one for work" came in a distant second at 11 percent. Third, at eight percent, was "mechanical problems with my current car." The remaining reasons, in order, were "special offer" (five percent), "new driver needs a car" (four percent), and "can afford one" (three percent). Note that both "special offer" and "can afford one" are based on wants as well. So if you compile all of these numbers, wants account for 44 percent of respondents' reasons for buying a new car; needs account for only 23 percent. Want trumps need nearly two to one.

Remember, we're talking about technical/scientific marketing here—cars fall into this category, and they're big-ticket items. You might *need* more contact lens solution, but, in most cases, you don't buy a new car unless you want one.

Appealing to Wants: A Case Study

Here's a compelling example of a case in which a technical marketer faced an uphill battle in trying to get customers to do what they "should" do by buying a product that met their needs—and the turnaround that happened when they shifted to a more wants-based marketing approach.

Dow AgroSciences, one of the world's leading producers of crop protection products, manufactures and markets a soil insecticide called Lorsban™ 15G. Lorsban can be used by peanut farmers to control several insects that damage peanut shells, which hurts the quality of the peanut and can allow a pathway for molds to get inside the shell and be harmful to people. This highly safe product is extremely effective when used properly. If there was ever a scientific and technical need for a product, this was it.

However, there were problems. Not scientific problems—marketing problems. Lorsban, a granular product, is applied after the peanut plants emerge from the ground. This requires application equipment not commonly available. In addition, research revealed that farmers considered the pests controlled by Lorsban to be seasonal; in wet growing seasons, they tended to cause problems, but not in dry years. Compounding this problem was the fact that most of these pests—lesser cornstalk borer, southern corn rootworm, wireworm, and cutworm—feed underground. If the farmers couldn't see them, they weren't there. Out of sight, out of mind.

The primary competition? No treatment at all. The vast majority of peanut acreage in primary peanut-growing states were not treated for these pests. And if farmers did treat, they tended to do so only after the problem reared its head. This created another less-than-desirable situation: Lorbsan did an excellent job of controlling pests when used as a preventive measure, but wasn't quite as effective as a rescue treatment. In other words, farmers who actually did use the product could be unhappy with the results.

Add up all the challenges, and Lorsban faced what you might think of as a marketer's worst nightmare: customers who largely don't understand how to use your product, don't buy it, and can be dissatisfied with it when they do.

What to do? Clearly, a repositioning of the product was in order. That's why Dow AgroSciences consulted me.

Enter wants-based marketing.

Lorsban had always been sold the way most crop protection products were sold: as a way to control pests. This is classic needs-based, feature-oriented technical marketing: "Our product controls pests, and you have pests you need to control, so you need our product and should buy it."

Farmers could certainly see value in controlling pests—when they had them, *and only as a means to an end*. The end was growing what peanut growers refer to as Segment 1 peanuts—the nice-looking, high-quality, high-value peanuts that consumers (and peanut buyers) prefer. At the time I undertook the project, growers were seeing a huge difference in prices paid for Segment 1 peanuts versus lower-quality Segment 3 peanuts: around $700 a ton for the former, only a little more than $100 for the latter. By controlling the insects that chew through peanut shells, Lorsban is extremely effective at helping farmers produce high-quality Segment 1 peanuts—when they apply it preventively.

If the Lorsban marketing team wanted to improve their efforts, they could have continued down the needs-based path into advantages ("Lorsban eliminates all these harmful pests from your crops") or even financial benefits ("Lorsban can help you make more money from your peanuts"). However, I didn't think the financial consideration, while strong, would have gotten to the heart of what farmers really wanted, and, in the process, would have made Lorsban sound like every other marketer claiming his product was going to improve profitability.

Wants-based marketing considers the end; remember, we're talking about what people care enough about to take action. What farmers really wanted was *to grow the peanuts that peanut buyers wanted to buy.*

This was the position I brought to the table, and the one Dow AgroSciences adopted for Lorsban. We backed it with an aggressive campaign to reach growers who were not currently using the product. We implemented a rebate program to encourage trial. We created literature informing Lorsban's audience that their dealers had applicators to apply the product, removing this barrier to purchase. We also created a video that included interviews with peanut buyers wherein they told growers exactly what they were looking for, and distributed the video free to interested farmers.

These are just a few broad highlights of a very thorough, well-researched program. But the primary point is that Lorsban repositioned itself around a wants-based message as opposed to the needs-based message they had been using.

The results? By appealing to what growers really wanted and targeting them with a consistent, powerful, wants-based message, Lorsban grew its peanut-grower customer base and reached growers who were farming more acres and using Lorsban on vastly more of their acreage, *inside of a single selling season.* Sales increases of nearly half the total were attributable directly to growers who saw and acted upon a wants-based marketing campaign.

The financial results? Those were strong, too. Assuming a typical customer retention rate for this category, no increase in acreage for retained farmers, and marketing spending of only one-third the first year's budget for each of the next four years of the campaign, the marginal rate of return per year, over five years, was nearly 137 percent. Compare that with the five-or-so percent they'd have realized if they'd invested their money in Treasury Bills. All marketing costs, direct and indirect, were paid back in about eight months.

Given this example, if you can't see how appealing to wants instead of needs pays off, you are nuts. Pun intended.

What Do *You* Want?

Is Lorsban an unusually strong example? Or will you experience similar dramatic results in your marketing program when you stop making the same mistake all the other technical marketers are making? I'd suggest that it's at least worth examining your marketing messages in the light of a wants-based approach.

And, my personal experience has taught that this sort of success is not unprecedented. In case after case, technical marketers who thought they had to reach their audiences with technical messages have been surprised to see how effective a wants-based message that appeals to emotions can be. This is particularly true if your product has some significant advantages over the competition. But it's an approach that's also effective if you're in a parity market. Again, take a page from the consumer marketers: beer is beer is beer, but one brand is best for making men attractive to women, another is for special occasions, another is the official beer of nightclubs, another is for active people, another is for people who really want something European . . .

You get the idea. People don't buy what they need. They buy what they want. And if what you want is a marketing program that works and makes you the rising star of your company, this is one common mistake you need to stop making today.

What Should You Remember from Reading this Chapter?

- ☞ **Need** may be the **most overused word** in technical marketing. It's also dangerous because it's thrown around haphazardly and it represents marketers who are out of touch with how and why their customers buy.

- ☞ Studies show people don't buy what they need. **People buy what they want**.[3]

- ☞ **Marketing is all about choice.** Which means it's about wants—not needs.

- ☞ **When it comes to selling, emotion—not logic—is primary** regardless of who you're selling to: men or women, physicists or psychics, engineers or English teachers.

- ☞ Within the classic features-advantages-benefits continuum, many technical and scientific marketing efforts start and end with features. **Benefits start to address what people want—and wants speak to emotion.**

- ☞ Wants-based marketing focuses on **what customers care enough about to take action.** Needs-based marketing isn't as effective as wants-based marketing.

- ☞ **Consumer and package good marketers** have long been masters of getting to what people really want. Technical marketers can learn a lot from them.

Brand Buster #2

Falling in Love with Your Product (Instead of Your Customer)

"LET ME TELL YOU a little bit about what you're getting into here," a prospective client once said to me. "We're selling a product to engineers, and engineers speak their own language. They're not interested in anything unless you can support it with data. You have to show them the data. Our ads have to be all about the facts. Fortunately, when you lay out the facts about our product, it's something that engineers really want."

I told this prospect I didn't think I agreed with him and that I wasn't certain I could help him. "Frankly, I'm not interested in doing marketing I don't think will work," I said. "You're starting with the assumption that engineers aren't like other people, and that emotion has no place in selling your product."

"You're exactly right," he said.

To which I said, "Yes, I am. I really *can't* help you."

It happens every day. Some very bright people in marketing departments think two things about marketing that are very wrong. The first is that their customers are somehow different from all the other people on the planet. The second is that their product is so wonderful that all you have to do is set it on a table in front of people and they'll beat down the doors to buy it.

Interestingly enough, though, engineers and doctors and CPAs and business owners and all sorts of people with scientific and technical jobs also respond to ads for Disney World, McDonald's, and

Toyota. And all sorts of great products lose out to lesser competitors who simply out-market them.

The fact is, all marketers are susceptible to the idea that their audiences are "different" and "special"—that they are somehow more sophisticated or specialized than other audiences and that lots of technical jargon is required to make the sale. Make no mistake: this is arrogant and dangerous thinking, focused not on what customers want, but on what the marketer wants to sell. At best, it leads to boring, nearly invisible marketing. At worst, it can actually damage your relationships with customers and prospects. *It can make them not want to buy your product.*

I call it "falling in love with your product instead of your customer." And if love is blind, it means you could be hurting your company without even knowing it.

Are You an Innovator?

Probably not. Most people aren't.

I don't mean by this that you don't have good ideas or that you don't sometimes—or even frequently—come up with unique solutions to problems. I'm talking about "Innovators" as a market segment, as discussed by Geoffrey A. Moore in his breakthrough book *Crossing the Chasm: Marketing and Selling High-Tech Products to Mainstream Customers.* (HarperBusiness, 1991) If you've worked in marketing for any time at all, chances are good you've already been exposed to this excellent book. If not, I highly recommend it.

Moore notes that every new technology goes through an adoption life cycle in which certain audience segments adopt the product before others are willing to do so. Moore didn't invent the life cycle adoption concept, but he did develop several new ideas that help marketers leverage the life cycle concept to their advantage.

Here's their take on things:

Innovators are the earliest adopters of new products. They're technology enthusiasts who need the latest and greatest. They like technology for technology's sake. They pursue new technology aggressively, learning about and evaluating new products in an effort to be first. They're likely to try anything new.

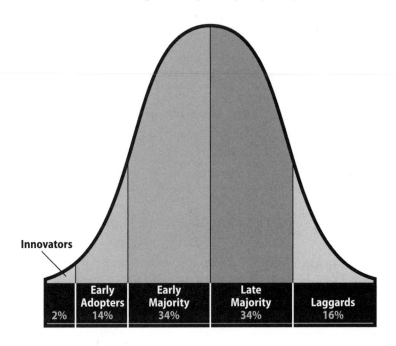

Technology Adoption Life Cycle

Every new technology goes through an adoption life cycle in which certain audience segments adopt the product offering before others are willing to do so.

You know Innovators. They're the people who had flat screen TVs in their homes when flat screen TVs still cost $15,000. They were the first folks on the block with a hybrid car.

Innovators are often the exception to the rule. Innovators may be so "up" on technology that you can appeal to them with an esoteric presentation of product features.

And Innovators are important. For marketers, they represent a beachhead, an important source of references and referrals. If you have Innovators using your product, it can be easier to introduce it to a larger audience.

But Innovators are also few in number. They represent only two to three percent of the overall market for a product. You simply can't hit a large target audience by trying to appeal to Innovators.

Another potential problem is that Innovators often get burned. Take video recorders. In the early days of home video technology, consumers had a choice of two tape formats: VHS and Beta. In many ways, Beta was the superior technology. Movies looked better when played on Beta machines. And the sound? Vastly superior to VHS.

However, most consumers couldn't detect the difference in picture quality between Beta and VHS, so the extra quality inherent in the Beta image really didn't matter. For most consumers it was the same for audio quality. However, Beta offered such superior audio quality to other audio playback devices that audiophiles routinely recorded their favorite music on videotape.

But VHS had some advantages of its own. For one thing, VHS tapes were two hours long, which meant that consumers could record a whole TV movie on one tape. Beta tapes were only an hour long, so you had to change tapes in the middle of the movie to get the whole thing.

When Beta machines were first introduced, they were also wildly more expensive than VHS machines, so consumers were asked to pay a lot more for very little discernable difference in quality.

Then there was the question of content. There were simply more movies available to rent or buy on VHS than on Beta. Better quality audio and video don't mean a thing if you can't watch what you want.

Today, of course, you can't find a Beta VCR (and very few VHS machines, either) in anyone's home. All those Innovators who bought Beta are now the proud possessors of some very expensive boat anchors, if they still have their tape machines at all.

And this is just one example of a marketer—in this case, Sony— falling in love with technology instead of its customers. (This, by the way, is unusual for Sony. Sony has a long and illustrious track record of knowing exactly what its customers want and giving it to them in a way they'll understand and buy.) Apple has been giving them a run for their money lately.

That Feature/Benefit Thing (Again)

In the last chapter, we talked about features and benefits and moving beyond them to wants. Again: features are what I need, benefits are what the features do for me, and *wants are what I care enough about to take action.*

You may also remember my telescope example. Here's an actual sample of copy from a telescope ad I saw in *Sky and Telescope*. (The manufacturer's name has been left blank and the model obscured, but you know who you are.) I know this will be difficult, but I'd like for you to read this copy in its entirety. As you read, try to figure out what it all means.

> The _____ 8″ Model X, with diffraction limited _____ optics in a computer-controlled telescope system, includes capabilities not available on other brands of 8″ Schmidt-Cassegrains costing hundreds of dollars more. Special features include: (a) a die-cast aluminum *double-tine* fork mount that rigidly supports the optical tube in all sky orientations; (b) *worm* gears of 4.9″-diameter on both telescope axes for smooth sidereal-rate tracking of celestial objects as well as precise guiding corrections during long-exposure imaging; (c) a rigid chromed-steel variable-height tripod—the same tripod provided with _____ more expensive models . . .

Are you kidding me? Can you use it to look at the moon?

This is an absolute classic example of marketers so in love with their products that the customer is nowhere to be found. There are plenty of features buried in that paragraph and even, if you have a lot of experience with buying telescopes, a benefit or two. But nowhere is there anything that addresses *wants*—the emotional reasons someone would actually want to buy a telescope.

The fact is, the marketing world—especially the technical/scientific marketing world—is clogged with messed-up brands marketed from the point of view of their creators. That can be frustrating for us as consumers. But it's not necessarily bad news for marketers. It means we have a real shot at putting out a message customers will understand and act upon.

Can You Bore Your Customer into Buying?

One of the most popular misconceptions in marketing circles is that "any advertising is good advertising." It's akin to the old show biz adage: "I don't care what they say about me, as long as they spell my name right."

This is the sort of wrong idea that commonly leads marketing people to create safe, boring advertising and marketing materials. If anything you put out there is going to work just as well as anything else, why in the world should you devote time and effort to your marketing?

Well, because it's simply not true. The smartest marketing people have known this for more than forty years.

Rosser Reeves was one of those smart marketing people. Reeves was one of the greatest advertising copywriters ever, the inventor of the unique selling proposition (USP) and the man whose creative brilliance helped turn Ted Bates & Company into one of the world's largest advertising agencies.

In Reeves' landmark book *Reality in Advertising* (Knopf, 1961) he addresses the subject of how the success of an advertising plan should be judged. Reeves suggests that people can be divided into two groups: those familiar with your advertising, and those unfamiliar with your advertising. These groups can then be subdivided into people who buy your product and those who do not. The important question is this: who buys more of your product? The people who know your advertising? Or the people who don't?

If any advertising was good advertising, it would stand to reason that, in virtually every case, people who knew your advertising would buy more than people who didn't. Reeves' surprising conclusion, however, supported with research data, was that there are many brands for which the exact opposite is true: more people who are unfamiliar with the advertising buy the product than people who know the advertising. This suggests a conclusion that is really a bit shocking: *your advertising can actually have a negative impact on your sales.*

This is not the place to delve into the reasons this situation may exist; suffice to say a campaign that's turning people off may involve bad marketing strategy, the wrong message, poor creative work, misguided media buying, or a combination of all of these factors. Here I'd like only to stress that not all marketing is good marketing, and that some marketing does more harm than good. As the great David Ogilvy once said, "You cannot bore your customers into buying your product." And boring, ill-conceived marketing is almost always the result of marketers who are in love with their products instead of their customers.

Quality and Other Great Big Nothings

What is "quality"? Believe it or not, it's a question that has driven people crazy, most notably Robert M. Pirsig, as witnessed in his classic book *Zen and the Art of Motorcycle Maintenance* (Morrow, 1974). This simple question turned a sane, relatively happy professor of philosophy into a barely functioning madman.

When it comes to marketing, "quality" has always driven me crazy, too, albeit in a much different way. Whenever their backs are against the wall, marketers who are in love with their products like to play the quality card. And, in most cases, all it ever leads to is bad marketing.

It goes like this: when asked to differentiate their product from competitors' products, marketers in love with their products will very often say, "We have superior quality." What exactly is this supposed to mean?

In one way, we all know what it means: our product is *better* than the other guy's. It's made better. Perhaps it will last longer. It will do a better job of whatever it's supposed to do.

All well and good. But quality is an empty word. What is "high-quality health care"? How is it different from regular health care? Quality is a word so vague and general that it is virtually meaningless.

Even more important, quality *always describes features*—and never addresses customers' wants. You don't want "quality health care." You want to feel better. You want to know that you don't have to worry about whether your doctors know what they're doing.

So why don't marketers come out and say these things? The smart ones do. The others are in love with their products. These marketers use lots of other relatively meaningless phrases, too. How many of these are you currently using?

- Excellent customer service
- Attention to detail
- Decades of experience
- Superior value
- Expertise
- Caring about your needs
- Exceeding your expectations

What's so shocking about this list is not that you see these words so commonly. What's truly shocking is that you see them so commonly with nothing tangible to back them up. In other words, more often than not, you'll see an advertiser claim "superior customer service," but not give you any reason to believe this may be true. In fact, you can create an entire ad using little more than the phrases above:

Headline:

Caring About Your Needs. Exceeding Your Expectations.

Copy:

Call on us. We combine decades of experience with proven expertise to provide you top quality products of superior value—and back them with excellent customer service and our reputation for strict attention to detail.

Are you laughing? If so, have you looked at your own advertising copy lately?

Talking Like a Real Person

It doesn't matter who you're trying to reach with your marketing message. You have to talk to customers just like you talk to your spouse and kids.

Because your customers are, in many ways, *just like your spouse and kids.* Depending on what you're marketing, your customers may actually *be* your spouse and kids. You don't talk down to them. You don't baffle them with BS. You speak compassionately and intelligently.

(If you're a stickler for grammar, you might also notice that I wrote "just like you talk to your wife and kids," instead of "just as . . . ," which is technically correct. That's because most people don't speak that way. More often than not, in the world of marketing communications, casual and conversational rule the day.)

Take a look at this example of an ad my agency created for a testing device that allows doctors to have young patients tested at home rather than at the doctor's office or lab. The headline says, "PT Testing Sounds Scary to Most Adults. Think How It Sounds to Her."

This ad created an emotional, empathetic appeal reminding physicians of the fear a child faces when visiting a doctor's office for a blood draw.

I happen to count a couple of doctors among my good friends. I can assure you doctors are people, too. The good doctors care deeply about their patients; the ones who care for children perhaps especially so. They know kids get scared. They realize how they act as doctors affects how their patients feel. Every decision they make, every instrument they purchase, makes a difference in the lives of their patients.

Do you think they'd rather do business with a company that understands this about them? Because the headline on this ad could have been something like, "Now . . . PT Testing At Home." But this doesn't begin to address what the doctor wants, which is to make the procedure less scary for the patient.

Here's what *Business Marketing* magazine said about this ad:

Roche Diagnostics effectively uses emotion to communicate to its target audience of cardiologists the benefits of a home testing kit for their young patients whose blood must be frequently measured for its thickness. The photo of the little girl with the soulful, penetrating stare will draw doctors into the ad. An interesting photo of a human face has enormous stopping power.[4]

Remember this last point. We're going to come back to it here, and we're going to examine it in greater depth in the next chapter. Before we do, though, I'd like to spend a little time on the elements of good copywriting: understanding your customer's pain and possibility.

There are two basic reasons people buy products, *any* products: to avoid pain and to capture opportunity. Think about it: you buy a car because you have places you want to go (opportunity) and you don't want to walk (pain). You buy toothpaste because clean teeth make you more appealing (opportunity) and save you the agony of dental repair (pain). You buy a new machine for your factory floor to take advantage of turning work you know is out there (opportunity) into income. You go to the doctor because you have a cough you can't shake (pain).

When we created the ad for Roche Diagnostics, we asked ourselves, "What pain does this product fix? What new possibilities or opportunities can it deliver?" We decided that doctors had the opportunity to make a scary situation far less painful for their patients—and ultimately, for themselves.

When you focus on pain and possibility, you naturally move beyond product features toward a better understanding of your customer. When you then craft verbiage that talks to your customer like a real person, you've taken a giant step toward creating the best kind of marketing message.

"But We Make Bearings!"

One more quick story: once upon a time, I had a client who made bearings for all sorts of automotive and industrial products. This client informed me right up front that bearings were, essentially, a commodity. All were priced just about the same, and one bearing manufacturer really wasn't all that different or better than the next. When asked why someone should buy their bearings, the marketing director replied, "Well, quality. Our quality is excellent."

Sigh.

Because it seemed like an interesting challenge, I took the assignment. I distinctly remember an early meeting with the client's marketing team, salespeople, and product engineers in which I was asked what I thought our ads would look like.

"I don't know," I said. "I won't know for quite some time; in fact, I'm not even sure yet that you should be running ads." We'd barely begun the discovery process. Ad design was about seventeen steps down the list.

"When you do need photos, though, we have them," said one of the engineers.

"I'm not sure we'll need them. If we do recommend ads, we might not want to use photos. We might not even want to show bearings," I said.

This last comment caused no small amount of sputtering among the salespeople. "But . . . we make bearings! We have to show what we make!"

"Do we?" I asked. "Let me ask you this: do your bearings look different from anyone else's?"

"No," said the marketing manager.

"So if we put a photograph of bearings in your ad, what good will that do you?"Even this difficult client had to admit, I had him there.

For the record, we ended up creating illustrations—not photographs—that featured bearings in highly unusual situations. The ads were distinctive and attention-getting, and gained this client a lot of inquiries from interested prospects.

The larger point here is that if you're selling bearings or medical equipment, what your product looks like is probably more related to features than to what your customer wants. Unless high design satisfies some kind of customer want for your product, a product shot front and center in your advertising probably says a whole lot less than you think it does.

What says more? Well, people's faces always say a lot. They're inherently interesting to us. They communicate emotion—which you'll remember is the key to customer wants.

Faces aren't always the best approach, of course. And we'll talk about design in more detail in the next chapter. Here, the point is that big product photos are often—dare I say, usually—a symptom of marketers who are in love with their products instead of their customers.

One final point from this little scenario before we move on: the marketing manager for the bearing manufacturer was, in my opinion, doing a little too much listening to the "experts" inside his company. The engineers who designed the bearings were naturally proud of their work, and naturally tended to focus on features. The salespeople dealt with customers every day, but they were as narrowly focused as the engineers—perhaps as a result of inadequate training. *Neither salespeople nor engineers who worked for the bearing manufacturer were actual customers.* As a marketer, it's important to have everyone's input. In other words, you may need love from all the people you work with, but when it's time to go to market, you have to have a monogamous relationship.

Love your customer. When you do, you'll usually find that your customer has good reasons to love you back.

What Should You Remember from Reading this Chapter?

☛ **Every new technology goes through an adoption life cycle** in which certain audience segments adopt the product offering before others are willing to do so.

☛ **Innovators are the earliest adopters of new products,** but represent only two to three percent of the overall market for a product. If you have Innovators using your product, it can be easier to introduce it to a larger audience.

☛ One of the **most popular misconceptions** in marketing circles is that **"any advertising is good advertising."** Studies show your advertising can actually have a negative impact on your sales.

☛ **You cannot bore your customers into buying your products.**

☛ **Commonly used words** and phrases such as "quality," "excellent customer service," "attention to detail," and "superior value" **always describe features—and never address customer wants.**

☛ There are two basic reasons **people buy products,** any products: **to avoid pain and to capture opportunity.**

☛ As a marketer, it's important to have everyone's (insiders) input. In other words, you may need love from all the people you work with. **But when it's time to go to market . . . love your customer.**

Brand Buster #3

Believing that Marketing is a Science or an Art

YOU REMEMBER THE STORY of the blind men and the elephant. Each blind man stood next to the elephant and was allowed to touch only one body part. Then each was asked to describe the elephant.

"An elephant is like a great tree trunk," said the blind man who touched the elephant's leg.

"No, no. An elephant is like a huge fan," said the blind man who felt the elephant's ear.

"You're both wrong," said the blind man who touched the elephant's trunk. "An elephant is coiled and slithering, like a serpent."

Needless to say, they were all only partially right, which is to say that they were all wrong. An elephant may have the attributes of a tree trunk, a fan, and a snake, but no one who could see the entire elephant would describe it in those terms.

Chapter 3, Lesson One: Marketing is an elephant.

A lot of marketers are of the opinion that marketing is a science. They believe in research and what it can tell them about their customers and prospects. They believe in creating marketing programs that are measurable. They're keen on attaching ROI to everything they do—and making changes when the results aren't up to snuff.

Still other marketers believe that marketing is an art. They see the artistry that goes into balancing media decisions and creating advertising and other marketing communications. They correctly understand that sometimes you just have to go with your gut instinct. They think that research is only going to tell them what they already know.

These marketers are all partially right. And all wrong.

Marketing contains elements of science that it would be foolish to ignore. Planning an ad schedule without researching your audience is just plain dumb. Marketing at its best also requires a certain artistry to push it beyond the ordinary and make it really special. There's nothing particularly scientific about creative risk-taking.

But in reality marketing is something else entirely. It's art and science—and something bigger that encompasses both.

We'll get to that in a little bit. First though, we're going to examine where our blind marketers get it right—before we blow holes in their marketing worldviews.

The Science in Marketing

Along about the time the Beatles first appeared on *The Ed Sullivan Show* came the first creative revolution in marketing and advertising. Led by Bill Bernbach of the advertising agency Doyle Dane Bernbach, the revolution inspired several generations of copywriters and art directors to push creative boundaries, to reach beyond easy solutions and develop ads that were intelligent, funny, and attention getting.

Sometimes it worked. Sometimes it didn't. Sometimes, lesser marketing minds, enamored of the artistic possibilities of this creative revolution, made marketing decisions that were just plain stupid. Some of them even thought that *any* advertising was good advertising.

They were wrong. As I mentioned in the previous chapter, at about the same time Rosser Reeves discovered that some advertising could actually make sales go down.[1]

Reeves who believed in measurement, knew better than to fall into the trap of thinking marketing was solely an art. On this topic he once said,

I'm not saying that charming, witty and warm copy won't sell.

I'm just saying that I've seen thousands of charming, witty campaigns that didn't. Let's say you are a manufacturer. Your advertising isn't working and your sales are going down. And everything depends on it. Your future depends on it, your family's future depends on it, other people's families depend on it. And you walk in this office and talk to me, and you sit in that chair. Now, what do you want out of me? Fine writing? Do you want masterpieces? Do you want glowing things that can be framed by copywriters? *Or do you want to see the . . . sales curve stop moving down and start moving up?* [1]

Kind of a no-brainer, isn't it?

The fact is, science should play a huge role in your marketing decisions because science can tell you so much about the things you need to know. Market research—whether you do it yourself (primary research) or find research that already exists (secondary research) can tell you an amazing number of things about your market, including:

Who your audience is. Why would you guess who's most likely to buy your product when a little research can tell you *exactly* who's going to buy? Today, the science of market research can tell, within a margin of error, where you shop for groceries, how much you spend, and what brands you buy, based on little more than your street address. If you're a business-to-business marketer, the information available to you is perhaps even more exact. For example, publications in some industries can provide you with lists of decision-makers, by job title, along with information about what they intend to buy and when they intend to buy it. If this information is available to you and you're marketing without it, you're flat-out wasting money.

What your audience responds to. Know how to find out what people like? Ask them. Focus groups and other research methods can tell you what people like and don't like about your company, your product, your advertising, and your competitors. In addition to asking, you can also observe the behavior of your customers and prospects. You can, for example, conduct eye motion studies that show exactly how readers look at print ads in magazines. (There's a pretty surprising study you'll learn about a little later on in the chapter.)

Your prospects' buying habits. How much do your prospects buy? When do they buy? Where do they make their decision? At their desks? Over a lunch conversation? When talking with a salesperson? Depending on what you're selling, there's an excellent chance that this information exists. If not, you can certainly commission a study to find out.

What ads they read and remember. Over the years, there have been thousands of studies performed detailing what ads readers remember. Scientists have studied how long the average reader looks at a magazine ad. Individual publications conduct readership studies all the time. They want you to keep advertising with them, so it's in their best interest to help you learn what works and what doesn't.

How much your product is worth to your customers. Think lowering your price will win you more customers? Before you answer, you should know that we're going to spend a whole chapter talking about the subject of pricing and the strategy of price-cutting. We're going to spend another whole chapter dealing with the question of whether your customers are really making buying decisions based on economics. Suffice to say at this point that market research really can give you a pretty good idea of what people are willing to pay for your product—no matter what your product is.

Your current reputation with customers. What do people really think about your product and your company? It seems self-evident, but lots of marketers don't take into account the fact that *people buy from companies they like and trust.* Consider your own buying experiences. If you're in the market for a new car, are you going to go to the dealer with the reputation for treating customers like idiots, or the one who treats customers fairly? Or think about insurance, a product no one actually likes to buy. Are you going to buy it from someone you like, or someone you can't stand to be around? In many cases, you may be willing to pay a premium price to buy from companies you like. For example, you may feel good about supporting a local bookseller, even though you know you can probably buy the same book online or from one of the chain stores for less money. The point here is that your reputation is critically important to your marketing, and research can tell you what your reputation is—and what it has to be to help you win more customers.

And I've only begun to scratch the surface of what science can do for marketers. Science can help you know your customers and create better, more effective ways to reach them. Clearly, marketing is a science. Right?

The Monster Question

Well . . . not so fast. All this research and science can be heady stuff. Which is exactly the problem.

It's easy to be seduced by science; just ask Dr. Frankenstein. As you'll recall, the good doctor cobbled together a monster out of a collection of body parts, just because he could, without regard for the "price." What he learned too late was that just because a thing could be done didn't necessarily mean it *should* be done.

Sometimes, marketers are tempted to play Dr. Frankenstein, too. They use bits and pieces of research in a way that leads to analysis paralysis—too much information, not enough intelligence, and no clear answers. You end up with a lot of elephant parts and no elephant.

You really *can* know exactly who your customers are, what they think, what they think about you, and what they want to buy. The answers are out there. And for a price, you can have them.

The question then becomes: what's the price?

The answer is: sometimes it's too high—in terms of both dollars and the messy monstrosity you create.

You have limited marketing dollars. The more dollars you use trying to figure out who you should be talking to and what they're buying, the fewer you have to actually reach your audience with your marketing messages. At what point do the costs of research and analysis outweigh the benefits? Are you better off doing a benchmark awareness study or running another flight of magazine ads? Is it really advisable to spend a bunch of money trying to determine the best places to spend your money?

Of course it is. To a point. You may have no hesitation about paying a financial planner for advice about saving for retirement. But investing even, say, ten percent of your savings in a financial planner's advice would seem absurdly high. Would you pay $10,000 to learn how to invest $90,000?

And, while we're asking questions we're not sure how to answer, how do you measure the impact of a good public relations plan? How do you measure the goodwill your industry grants you from your sponsorship of a trade event? Can you be sure it's worth what you're spending? And, if so, how much more is it worth to measure the cost so that you know for sure?

Confusing, isn't it? Especially since the answer to all of these questions is: it depends.

Believe It or Don't

It depends. It depends on your budget and the specific problem you need to solve and the depth and prickliness of that problem. It depends on how much the answer would sway your decisions in one direction or another. It depends on your current knowledge: do you think you have a good handle on what your customers want from you, or do you really not have any idea whatsoever?

Some years ago, I visited with a prospective client whose product was, essentially, a fundraising program for elementary schools and youth sports programs across the U.S. He wanted me to help him create a marketing plan that would raise awareness of his product and help him sell it to his prospects—most of whom were either the fundraising directors of their youth leagues or the presidents of their local parent-teacher organizations. His goal was to do a million dollars in sales in his territory. He had what he thought was a great product. He was motivated. He was prepared to spend some money to get it in front of his prospects. And this was not a product that was going to sell itself through ads or mailers. He *had* to get in front of his prospects to sell it.

But he had a basic problem: he didn't know how to reach them.

As it turns out, there was an organization of all the PTO presidents in the state. But that organization didn't rent its list of names to marketers. Individual schools didn't like to give out the names of their PTO presidents; they usually suggested my prospect leave his name in the hope that the PTO president would call *him*. That, obviously, was putting the success of his marketing program entirely in his prospects' hands. And that didn't make sense.

What should I have advised him to do? In this instance, I had no choice but to suggest some fairly extensive research into the best ways to reach his audience because the other factor my prospect had to face was that PTO presidents turn over every year. Even if he could develop a prospect list for this year, he was going to have to start over next year. So he really did need to spend some money up front before he went out to market his product.

Specifically, it made great sense to conduct a small-scale program of in-depth, qualitative interviews to ask prospects what they wanted. According to a study from MIT and the University of Chicago, in-depth interviews with as few as 12 or 15 randomly selected customers can represent an entire market segment with surprising accuracy.[2] These interviews can help you identify customer needs, help you understand your product's value in the marketplace, and predict marketplace behavior. In fact, these kinds of customer interviews, each lasting an hour or so, can be more cost effective and provide a greater depth of information than a comparable series of focus groups.

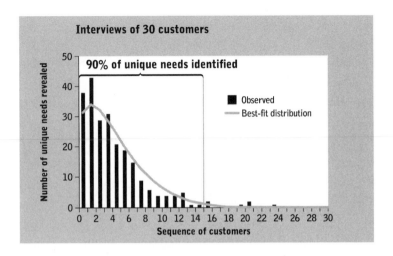

Handful of interviews reveals nearly all unique customer needs

MIT and University of Chicago researchers interviewed 30 prospects for portable food carrying devices (coolers, picnic baskets, etc.). Seven analysts (some experts and some with minimal training) then coded the transcripts to identify specific customer needs and which customers revealed them first. The first 15 customers interviewed identified more than 90% of unique needs.

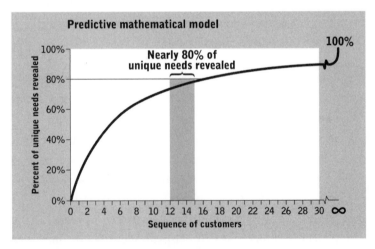

The researchers then developed a mathematical model based on the best-fit distribution to predict the percentage of customer needs a given number of one-hour interviews would reveal for a larger population. According to the model, it takes only 12 to 15 interviews to reveal nearly 80% of unique needs, regardless of the size of your market. Returns diminish quickly as the number of respondents increases.

As an aside, I'm not a big fan of focus groups. The big advantage is that you can get more opinions for less cost than doing individual interviews. But there's a tradeoff. People behave differently in groups than they do in person, and have a great propensity to either dominate the conversation or get bullied into submission to the will of the group. A good facilitator can help you get valuable information from a focus group, but the problems remain. I believe it's easier and more efficient to get your intelligence from personal interviews.

So, in some cases, primary research is critical. But I would suggest that my PTO prospect is an exception. Let's say for a moment that you're starting a business to make bicycle seats for sale to bike manufacturers; you're thinking about selling to consumers through bike shops someday, but for now, you're a business-to-business marketer. Like my prospect with the fundraising program, you hope to do about a million dollars in sales each year—and let's say you figure you have about $80,000 to put into marketing.

You know you have a great product. You know your cyclist pals prefer it; it's more stylish and more comfortable than the seats that come standard on the bikes they buy. You know you have your manufacturing and distribution processes in place, and you have a pretty good idea about what bike manufacturers are willing to pay for seats. You know exactly who these bike companies are.

How are you going to spend your $80,000?

Are you going to test the brand name you come up with? The ad you create? Are you going to find out exactly why these companies are buying what they're buying now? Are you going to test the relative merits of style, price, comfort, performance, and durability? Because if you are, you'll spend that $80,000 awfully quickly.

I would submit that, if you are committed to being in the bicycle seat business and you have $80,000 to spend on marketing, you ought to invest it in communications and sales materials. You might want to investigate the secondary research to see if there's anything else out there to confirm what you believe. But I think the situation comes down to one, simple choice: believe it or don't.

Simply put, you can believe that you have a pretty good handle on the way your business works and the way you should go to market, or you can decide you really don't know. If you really don't know, it's time to do some research.

Otherwise, I suggest that you develop a "reasonableness test" when it comes to research. If the research findings would be nice but not necessary and are going to seriously tap into the dollars you have to spend to market your product, don't do it. All other things being equal, put a limit on how much you'll spend on market research. Grow your business first. Then the more successful you are, the more you can refine your success with market knowledge.

The Marketing Laboratory

So how do you employ science responsibly? Here are a few tips:

Use what's out there. Marketing isn't exactly a new discipline. In one form or another, it's been around since . . . well, since the world's oldest profession. There's all kinds of secondary research available to tell you what you want to know. Publications in your industry are great storehouses of information. Often they have extensive market research available to their advertisers and prospects, some at little or no cost—perhaps a few thousand dollars, which can be vastly less expensive than the cost of collecting data yourself, if you can do it at all. You'll find all sorts of interesting resources online, too—try the American Marketing Association (*marketingpower.com*), the Institute for the Study of Business Markets at Penn State University (*smeal.psu.edu.isbm*), the Marketing Science Institute (*msi.org*), mediapost.com, marketingprofs.com, market-research.com, and marketingsherpa.com.

Take advantage of special offers. While we're on the subject of trade publications, you should know that magazines often conduct readership studies and other industry research that can give you excellent information about how well your ad is working—especially in comparison with other ads in your industry and your product category. These studies are available to advertisers at little or no additional cost. Why not take advantage of them?

Read your own trade journals. You might be surprised at the depth of research available to you through such publications as the *Journal of Marketing, Journal of Marketing Research, Journal of Advertising, Journal of Advertising Research,* and others. Such as? Read on. We're going to go into some depth about one study later on in this chapter.

And while you're at it, crack a few books. Start with *Scientific Advertising,*[3] written by Claude Hopkins and published in 1923—and still as vital today as the day it was published. According to the late, great ad man David Ogilvy, "Nobody should be allowed to have anything to do with advertising until he has read this book seven times. It changed the course of my life."

Ask your customers. You really don't have to go to a lot of extra effort to ask your own customers about their buying habits, what they like, how they make their decisions, and so forth. Customer feedback or product registration forms, inexpensive mail surveys, telephone follow-up, and other strategies can give you all sorts of valuable information at a minimal cost. In the front of this book you'll find several excellent books on conducting market research.

 Experiment. This is exactly how direct response writers have honed their craft over the years. Have you ever noticed tiny classified ads in the back of a publication you read that never seem to change—ads that appear exactly the same, month after month, year after year, even decade after decade? Those ads work. That's why they're there. Chances are, they were tested under real-world circumstances and refined until they pulled in customers reliably each month. You can test your advertising this way, too. The web is often a great way to do this.

Also, there's one final thing you ought to remember about science and advertising, and that's the fact that *people make purchase decisions based on emotion, not logic.* Your customer is not a computer. He or she accepts more than raw data as input.

The Art of Advertising

So now that we've built up and knocked down marketing as a science, let's look at the other side. What's wrong with thinking about marketing as an art?

Well, nothing. To a point. There is certainly a lot of artistry in marketing, particularly in advertising and other marketing communications. Plenty of people with "art" backgrounds find careers in marketing, and marketing firms and ad agencies hire lots of writers and designers—fields most of us would consider to be "the arts." In ad agencies, we even call them "art directors" and "creative directors." So even if marketing isn't an art, what about advertising—certainly one of marketing's chief functions—as art?

It's worth considering. In fact, it's worth taking a quick look at the elements of advertising to see the artistry involved in their creation.

The visual. Lots of advertising types would argue that the visual element of an ad—and by extension, of a brochure, website, or other communication—is the single most important element for engaging the reader. These arguments would certainly have some merit. We're drawn to visuals, certainly to visuals that are unusually beautiful or terrible or meaningful. We love faces in particular, which is why so many ads feature big pictures of human faces. Ad agency art directors can spend many days and thousands, even tens of thousands of dollars, creating a single image designed to draw you into an ad. There is certainly a lot of artistry involved.

The copy. Lots of other advertising types would argue that copy is king. They would tell you that ads are, after all, meant to communicate a message, and you usually need words to get the message across. Most ad agency owners and creative directors would also tell you that hiring good copywriters is one of their most challenging problems. There's an art to copywriting, they'll tell you. Not everyone can do it. In fact, most people can't.

The design. The true artistry in advertising and other marketing communications may reside with the design that takes all of the elements—the visual, the headline, the body copy, and the logo—and makes of them a unified whole that speaks to the audience. Advertising design is a tricky and delicate balancing act. (Or is it? Stay tuned. We're going to take a close look at this issue in the next section.)

The production. Just as the designer takes all the elements of an ad or brochure and turns them into something more than the sum of their parts, so the producer creates television and radio commercials or video or audio podcasts that combine art direction, scriptwriting, acting, music, and all sorts of other elements. It no longer shocks us to understand that many of the thirty-second television commercials that run in prime time cost more to produce than the programs they sponsor. Most of us would concede that film is an art form. Is it any less so if it's only thirty seconds long?

Of course, we're just scratching the surface of the artistic elements in advertising and marketing. And remember, as we discussed in Chapter One: people make buying decisions with their hearts, not their heads. To touch the heart you need art, not science.

The End of the Art?

Recently, I came upon a fascinating study that had to do with the relationship among elements in print ads.[4] I was surprised to learn that, whereas print ads had been studied for many years and researchers had long used sophisticated devices to track eye movement on a page to see exactly what readers are looking at and how long they're looking, no one had ever studied the effect of the relative size and prominence of the different parts of the ad: specifically, the visual, the copy, and the logo.

Maybe it had never been studied because it's so easy for any good creative director to tell you the results before you do the research. Big pictures attract readers. People don't read copy, so use as little as possible. Using a big logo makes your ad look horsy, and instantly screams, "This is an ad!" And people don't buy magazines to look at the ads, so as soon as they see the logo, it's a signal to turn the page. Most advertising creatives agree, then: big picture, short copy, small logo.

What's interesting is that one study showed almost exactly the opposite results. Researchers found that, indeed, the pictorial element in the ad was important for capturing attention, and that it was important *regardless of size*. An increase in the size of the picture *did not* increase attention to the ad as a whole; small pictures worked just as well as pictured that dominated the page.

What about the text, then? Surely the tests confirmed the well-known fact that people don't read copy, and that a big copy block is an instant turn-off. Right?

Well, no. The study found that increasing the amount of space devoted to text in the ad actually increased attention to the ad.

Ads for high-involvement products—that is, products for which readers said the buying decision was important—especially benefited from having more space devoted to text. And if readers were familiar with the product being advertised, having a lot of text prompted them to pay closer attention—even though they were less inclined to pay attention to ads for familiar products as a whole. Strike two.

The last point has to be upheld though, doesn't it? Small logos simply must be better than big ones.

Except that they're not. According to the study, when the logo attracts attention, it serves to transfer the reader's attention to the other parts of the ad. In other words, when the logo attracts attention, readers pay more attention to both the picture and the text.

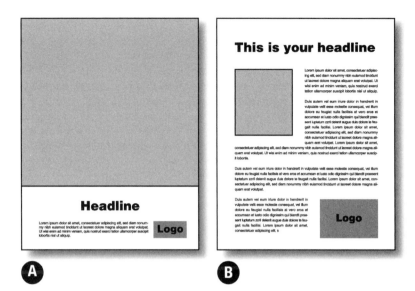

Which ad will attract more readers?

According to one study, the answer is Ad "B" because it has more copy and it has a larger logo (brand element). Don't be fooled by the large photo in Ad "A." Having a picture is important. The size of the picture isn't.

Put it all together, and this study seems to be saying that the more aesthetically pleasing you try to make your ads, the less effective they are. Small pictures, lots of copy, and a big logo may work best of all.

And this was no small study. Researchers studied data from 33 independent eye-tracking tests of print advertisements in 65 magazines with a total sample of more than 3,600 consumers and ads for 812 national and international brands in 71 product categories.

Another interesting bit of news from the study: on average, magazine readers spent only one more second looking at editorial content than at advertising; ads were looked at for 1.73 seconds, editorial for 2.79 seconds. So don't believe a "browsing" reader won't notice your ad. *Most* readers are browsers and your ad *will* get noticed, if it's the right kind of ad.

More About What Makes a Good Print Ad

So the study said people gazed at ads for an **average** of 1.73 seconds. That is, of all the ads studied, that's how long readers looked on average at every ad, but they spent considerably longer than 1.73 seconds with some ads. Yet for others, *they never even gazed upon them.* Ouch!

Hearing this, my mind (and maybe yours) immediately jumps to another important question: "How likely is it a magazine reader will see *my* ad at all?"

To that end, a German eye movement tracking study revealed *eye contact is made with approximately 90 percent of all print advertisements* of three-quarters of a page or larger.[5]

Fascinating, huh? Hold on: it gets even more interesting.

Ordinarily, when you ask people if they have seen any particular ad, about 60 percent say yes. But with the German study saying people truly look at 90 percent of the ads, what happened to the missing 30 percent (the people who really did see the ad, but say they didn't)?

Erik DuPlessis, in his book *The Advertised Mind* (Kogan Page, 2005) takes a crack at the answer. He cites a NIPO study in which readers reported seeing 70 percent of the ads they looked at. (Hmmmm . . . using the 90 percent "gazed at" German number, times the 70 percent "seen" number, my calculation equates to readers saying they saw 63 percent of the ads [.90 x .70]—about what we see in most studies of ad recall/recognition. Pretty cool, huh?) DePlessis goes on to tell us the majority of the difference between what readers "gaze at" versus report as "seen" can be attributed to *how long* they look at the ad. Observation time for ads not remembered "was less than 0.75 seconds." Ads looked at and reported as seen "had to have been viewed for longer than 2.75 seconds."

Now we get to the point. You need readers to spend time with your ads if you want them to register. Which leads us back to the reason it's so important to include a picture, a big logo, and enough copy to tell the story. But that's just the mechanics. What about the content?

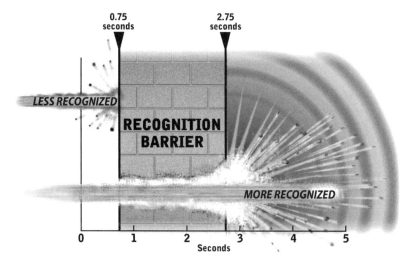

Breaking the recognition barrier

Observation times play a critical role in ad recognition and recall. Ads viewed 0.75 seconds or less did not break the recognition barrier, and therefore were less recognized. Ads viewed 2.75 seconds or longer broke through, resulting in higher recognition.

A European study conducted by Medialogue (Stop|Watch, 2005) summarizes around 300,000 observations of general consumers to nearly 3,000 print advertising campaigns.[7] (As an aside, I'd rather use studies from technical/scientific trade publications, but none of this type or magnitude exists. Can consumer results be perfectly correlated to the technical and scientific world? No. Can I draw some useful conclusions? I believe so. People are people. We respond psychologically in similar ways whether at work or at home. Human behavior is pretty much human behavior, and it's been this way for hundreds, if not thousands, of years. I still laugh at Shakespeare's comedies. Don't you?)

Back to the Stop|Watch study: effective print advertising boiled down to four factors. Is the ad:

1. Likeable?

2. Original?

3. Informative?

4. Suited?—to the environment of the publication. (A motor oil ad in a cooking magazine isn't well-suited.)

The most effective ads scored well on these factors overall on a scale of 1 to 10. By "effective" the study meant the ad achieved higher scores on two factors: recognition and attribution. Recognition is the percentage of people who report having seen an ad when shown the actual ad (minus any of its brand or product name elements). Attribution is the percent of people who correctly identify the brand or product being advertised for any ad they report having seen. Ad-liking turns out to be the most important factor affecting these results. Eighty percent of the variation in recognition and 51 percent of the variation in attribution can be linked to ad-liking. So, of all the factors, ad-liking turns out to be the 800-pound gorilla. (For lots more details about this fascinating study, I refer you to the complete report, available online at: *www.ppamarketing.net/public/downloads/Stopwatch_everything_on_magad_impact.pdf*)

So what about *your* print advertising? You can begin improving it immediately by focusing on factors one through three above. (I'm going to assume your ads are "suited" to the publications you run them in.) Understand what your audience likes—not just in their advertising, but in general. If you don't know what they like, find out. Use the individual interview technique I described earlier in this chapter. Same goes for originality and what constitutes "informative" to your audience. Then infuse what you've learned into your advertising. And finally, test your proposed advertising before you run it. You can hire a market research firm to do a copy test, or you can roll up your sleeves and do it yourself. For those of you who want to do it yourself, here's my suggested approach for conducting a qualitative ad test. (Remember, I'm a big believer in qualitative research.)

DIY Print Ad Testing Guide

What follows are some general guidelines for conducting a print ad test. I've also included a "tee-up" or introduction that will help you explain to participants how the ad testing will be done and what you expect of them.

How-to Tips

Test widely divergent concepts. *Do* test several completely different big ideas, messages and/or executions—a people/testimonial ad vs. a long copy technical data ad vs. a big visual/billboard ad with hardly any copy, and so forth. *Don't* test minor differences—for instance, one ad with three different background colors.

Conduct one-on-one interviews, in person, maybe at a trade show or industry conference. Pay your subjects or give them a gift/incentive for participating (if you must).

Choose participants that represent your audience. Don't interview sales people; they're not your audience.

Test at least two and no more than four ads.

Size matters—try to complete 12 to 15 interviews.

Alter order of the ads, i.e., mix up the sequence in which you present the ads to participants.

Gather this information for each interview:

Date
Participant Name
Ad Sequence (A, B, C – B, C, A, and so forth)

Take good notes, especially of their comments related to feelings/impressions (trust me—you'll forget later who said what).

Probe for deeper answers, i.e., ask participants, "Why did you say that" or "Explain that to me."

Don't ask participants which ad is their favorite/best or which they think is going to work the best. You're the marketer; figuring that out is your job.

Don't ask participants if the ad is believable. I've found this question just doesn't work. To start with, the setting is unbelievable. Nobody hands a reader an ad and says, "Read this." If something strikes them as not credible, it will come up by asking the questions below.

Ad Testing Tee-Up with Participant

Open the interview like this:

"I'm going to hand you several ads, one at a time. When I hand you the first ad, I will ask you to read it. When you have finished reading the ad, I will begin by asking you several questions. When we are finished with those questions, I will hand you the next ad. After we've finished with all the ads, I'm going to ask you some general questions."

Then hand out the first ad. (Lather, rinse, and repeat until you're done.)

Here's What You Ask

Now for the questions. I've broken them into two categories: Ad Questions and General Questions. The Ad Questions should be read for each ad. Remember to mix up the order in which participants review each ad. When all the Ad Questions are completed, proceed to the General Questions.

Ad Questions

1. What are your feelings and reactions after reading this ad?

2. What about this ad appeals to you the most? Please explain.

3. What about this ad appeals to you the least? Please explain.

4. Did anything confuse you in this ad? Please explain.

5. Rate this ad on a scale of 1 to 10 for

   - How well you like it: 1 = hate it; 10 = love it

   - How original it is: 1 = not at all original; 10 = never seen anything like it before

   - How informative it is: 1 = not at all informative; 10 = outstanding, lots of good information

General Questions (after they have viewed all the ads)

1. What are your impressions of the company?

2. What would you tell a colleague this company/product does?

Finally, ask specifically about anything else you're unsure of or there is debate about in your camp, such as reactions to a key visual or tag line, interpretation of a chart or graph, or familiarity of the audience with specific terms or words used in the copy.

Interpreting the Results and Taking Action

Be clear on the objective of the ad. Agree within your group (or in your mind) on the exact purpose *before* you begin analyzing results. (This should be no big deal, since you should have nailed down the objective way before you created the ads!) Base your analysis of the results against the objective.

Don't get hung up on the numbers. Several of my questions do use a number scale, but your sample size isn't big enough for numerical differences to be valid.

Use your critical thinking skills instead. Look at all the input you've gathered and then answer the question, "Which best achieves the objective?" Digging deeper, did you find general agreement in certain areas? Any disagreement or confusion? (Confusion is the kiss of death with a print ad. Remember, readers on average spend less than two seconds with your ad. Confuse them in that time and you've blown it.)

Resist the temptation to combine all the best elements of all the ads into one "super" ad. It won't work. Remember how the "Dr. Frankenstein approach" to research didn't work? It doesn't work for creative execution, either. (You'll probably ignore my advice on this point once or twice. Please remember I warned you.) Focus instead on smoothing out the problem areas with the "winning" ad.

So is this all there is to ad testing? Heck no. Loads of market research companies can give you a much more comprehensive approach. But my method will provide you with some useful direction to help you make better decisions about your print advertising. Give it a try.

What does this all mean? Clearly, it has implications for advertisers who want people to pay attention to their ads. But for our purposes here, it means that maybe advertising—that most artistic function of marketing—isn't an art, either. Because when you take all of those artistic elements and make them look as "artful" as possible, you actually may be hurting your marketing effort. That's what science seems to be telling us, anyway.

And it's an incredibly important point. Far too many marketers—smart, savvy marketers—get hung up on creating art for art's sake and forget that they're actually supposed to be marketing a brand. How many times has it happened that you've seen a TV commercial that's absolutely hilarious—so funny, in fact, that you have to tell your friends or your spouse about it? And while you're in the middle of telling them about the commercial, you realize you don't know what brand is being advertised? You know it's a beer or a car or batteries, but you have no idea who the advertiser might be.

It happens all the time. The creative approach—the art—overwhelms the marketing. And the marketer's good sense.

Build the Sandbox and Let Them Play

So now we've admitted there's art in marketing. But we've also seen that marketing is not exactly an art, and that art can actually get in the way of communication. How, then, are we supposed to put art in perspective?

First, we have to realize that marketing does, in fact, attract creative people with artistic abilities. They are drawn to art and to using their talents artfully. These people are invaluable in any marketing organization: we need them. Without them, we can't hope to reach our audiences powerfully and persuasively.

What we must do is provide them with the best direction we possibly can in terms of who we're trying to reach, what we need to say, and what we want our audience to do. The art comes in the execution, not in the basic planning.

I like to use the analogy of playing in the sand. Telling your creative team to come up with a great marketing idea without the proper direction is like dropping them in the middle of the Sahara and asking them to make a sandcastle. It's too big. The possibilities are too wide-open. The landscape is too vast; chances are good they're going to build something that's either irrelevant or invisible.

It's a lot better if you build them a sandbox. You don't care what kind of castle they build as long as it fits inside the box; that is, as long as it meets your objectives. And, sure: they can *think* outside the box. But they have to execute *inside.* That is, the wild idea must meet the objective, or it's not just a wild idea, it's a bad idea.

Speaking of ideas, I would suggest to every reader that *ideas* are the source of true artistry in marketing. These days, ideas are getting scarce. It's pretty easy to use today's computer technology to make ads and brochures and Web sites and other communications look nice. But great design never made up for a bad idea.

So What Is It?

Marketing incorporates elements of science, and science can do a lot for marketers, but marketing is not a science—and looking at marketing as a science may cost too much, and may suck the soul out of your marketing messages. Marketing makes use of art and artistry, but marketing is not an art—and looking at marketing as an art can cause you to create attractive promotions that nevertheless do not actually help you sell anything.

So if marketing is not an art and not a science, then what is it?

Well, I hate to be so very elementary, but Merriam-Webster defines marketing as "the process or technique of promoting, selling, and distributing a product or service." In other words, for the most part, marketing is about *selling*. And selling is something that can make the scientists and artists among us cringe with embarrassment.

Marketing, we hope, leads to selling. In fact, you could probably get into a fairly lengthy and pointless argument about whether sales is a subset of marketing or marketing is a subset of sales. The answer has more to do with individual corporate hierarchies and org charts than it has to do with reality. It's *all* related to getting the word out about your product and getting that product into people's heads and hands. I have long held that the true job of marketing is to make products easier for customers to buy and easier for companies to sell.

So those of us who come from the creative side of the business—remember, I began my marketing career as a copywriter—have to get over ourselves and understand that we're not creating art: we're salespeople whose tools are words and pictures, not briefcases and firm handshakes. Those who come from the scientific side of the business have to get over themselves, too. You have to allow the creativity that will touch people's emotions and compel them to take action—and you have to understand that sometimes effective selling just doesn't require the depth of scientific understanding that may be possible in any given situation.

Marketing, in the end, is the Middle Way: part art, part science, all salesmanship. Veer too far in one direction, and you become silly and irrelevant. To paraphrase Rosser Reeves, do you want art, or do you want the sales curve to go up? Veer too far in the other, and you become costly and boring. To paraphrase David Ogilvy, nobody ever bored the customer into buying anything.

Or to go back to the story we opened with, marketing is the elephant—the *whole* elephant. Close your eyes to its essence, and you'll never really understand it. Open your eyes and you may be surprised at its power.

What Should You Remember from Reading this Chapter?

- ☞ **Marketing is something bigger than art or science** that encompasses both.

- ☞ Merriam-Webster defines marketing as: **the process or technique of promoting, selling and distributing a product or service.**

- ☞ Science should play a huge role in marketing decisions. **Market research can tell you an amazing number of things** about your audience, your product's worth to that audience, your company's current reputation, whether or not your current campaign is working, and more.

- ☞ Marketers with limited marketing dollars should consider **at what point the costs of research and analysis outweigh the benefits**.

- ☞ In-depth interviews with **as few as 12 or 15 randomly selected customers can represent an entire market segment** with surprising accuracy. These interviews can be more cost effective and provide a greater depth of information than a comparable series of focus groups.

☞ Recent research showed **an increase in the size of the picture didn't increase attention to the ad** as a whole. The study found increasing the amount of text in the ad actually increased attention.

☞ Studies show that to **be effective, print advertising needs to be like-able, original, informative and suited to the environment** of the publication.

☞ Far too many smart, savvy **marketers get hung up on creating art for art's sake** and forget they're actually supposed to be marketing a brand.

Brand Buster #4

Trying to Please Everyone

HERE'S AN INTERESTING and enlightening exercise: take a couple of minutes this week to find a listing of the most popular songs on the radio for the year you were a senior in high school.

For the sake of this exercise, let's pick 1975—a late Baby Boom graduation year. Here were some of the most popular songs of that year:

"Another Somebody Done Somebody Wrong Song"
   —B.J. Thomas

"Bungle In The Jungle" —Jethro Tull

"Convoy" —C.W. McCall

"Feelings" —Morris Albert

"Holy Roller" —Nazareth

"The Hustle" —Van McCoy

"Laughter in the Rain" —Neil Sedaka

"Love Will Keep Us Together" —Captain & Tenille

"My Eyes Adored You" —Frankie Valli

"That's The Way (I Like It)" —KC & the Sunshine Band

"Who Loves You" —The Four Seasons

"Wildfire" —Michael Murphey

These are not on many people's lists of timeless pop classics. Some (okay, most) were pretty darn bad. Nor are these the artists who will be remembered as the top acts in their pop music sub-genres. And even if you like one or more of these artists, these songs—which were, remember, big hits—were almost certainly not their best work.

So why were these all such big hit songs? One reason: because, although they were created to appeal to large segments of people, they weren't created to appeal to *everybody*.

Maybe *you* didn't like "Wildfire," but millions of other pop music fans did; in fact, since 1975, "Wildfire" has been played on radio and television more than *four million* times, making it one of the most played songs ever.

Now, we don't consider Michael Murphey a giant in the world of popular music. He's not up there with the Beatles or the Rolling Stones.

When you think about it, though, Michael Murphey was a pretty good marketer. Here's why. Some people (like me) hated that song. In fact, I'd wager that millions upon millions of people disliked it and still do. But a fraction of a percent of the public loved it. And in a market like music, that's all it takes to be a top seller. Is there a lesson here for us? Yes.

Michael Murphey, whether he knew it or not, avoided our Brand Buster #4—the mistake of trying to please everyone—and rode his acumen in music and marketing to the top of the charts.

Lots of people never do understand this lesson. And it's for good reason. It's because a lot of people come into a marketing role from the world of sales. Arriving on the job, they don't understand that the role of marketing is as much about "no" as it is about "yes." This is a foreign concept to most people with a sales background. But when you're in marketing, you have to embrace the idea that you can't please everyone and you make more money when you stop trying.

Yet I've seen many marketers insist that everyone in their product category should be interested in buying their product. So they go to market with messages designed to appeal to everyone: the prospect who buys on price, the one who buys on high performance, the one who cares most about dependability, the one who is looking for the most high-tech features, the one who wants only the latest and greatest, and so on. In trying to appeal to everyone, these marketers weaken their message to the point that they end up appealing to no one.

To put it another way, there's no shame in being the Michael Murphey of marketing. If you'd like to learn how, read on.

How to Light a Fire Under Your Customers

Any tenderfoot scout worth his merit badges can tell you the way to start a fire is not to spread your embers all over the yard. If you really want to generate some heat, you consolidate your embers in a small fire pit.

And any swami worth his meditation pillow can tell you that it's easy to sleep on a bed of nails; your weight is distributed evenly over all of the little points, so they don't penetrate your skin. But you can't sleep on a single nail. Without any other support, you're too heavy. You're looking at a bad puncture wound (and probably a tetanus shot).

On the other hand, as a marketer, you're trying to poke into your prospect's consciousness. You don't want your prospect to fall asleep on all those little points: you want your sharpest, tallest nail to make the strongest impression possible, so your prospect will remember you.

And, just so we keep as many metaphors in the air as possible (we've got pop music and nails floating up there nicely), the right way to light a fire under your best prospects is not to diffuse your energy. In marketing, it means finding out the strengths of your brand that really resonate with your customers and making the most of them. That means being willing to say "no"—by refusing to load your marketing communications with ancillary points that don't matter to most of your audience.

This isn't just my opinion. According to a recent study, simple ads are more compelling and believable, and have a greater "Truth Effect" than ads with more complicated messages.[1]

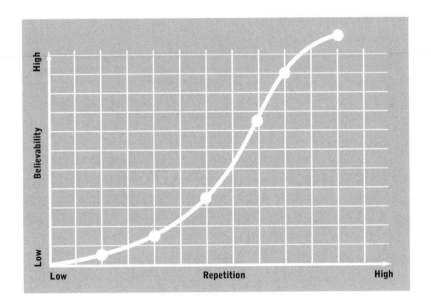

The Truth Effect

Good things happen when you repeat yourself. Studies show frequency of repetition increases the believability of simple advertising messages. Marketers refer to this phenomenon as the "Truth Effect."

In this study, over the course of two sessions, researchers exposed 237 subjects to advertising claims, some true and some false. Subjects saw some claims only in the first session, some only in the second session, and some in both sessions. One group of subjects was asked to gauge the truth or falsity (yes, that's a real word) of the claims on a seven-point scale from "definitely false" (1) to "definitely true" (7). Another group rated whether the messages were easy to understand, from "difficult to understand" (1) to "very easy to understand" (7).

The results? When researchers asked both groups whether they believed the claims in the ads, subjects reported claims they encountered more than once were more believable—whether these claims were actually true or false. (We'll talk more about the importance of frequency in Chapter 5: Forgetting That People Forget.)

But the subjects in this study reported another interesting fact as well. The other factor measured in this study had to do with "involvement" with the ads; that is, when test subjects were asked to judge the truth or falsity of ad claims, they became more involved with the ads. The more involved the subjects became, the more skeptical they were of the claims being made. In other words, if you make a lot of claims in your ads, you're inviting greater skepticism than if you make just one, strong claim.

Based on decades of personal experience as a marketer, I would also suggest to you that another problem with most advertising is that it tries to close the sale in one shot instead of inviting *awareness* and *consideration.* You can't sell a product unless you have a prospect considering your product for purchase. And you can't have consideration until you have basic awareness. You might think of your customer's mind as a continuum in terms of ever-narrowing "sets": from the "universe set" of all companies (including you and all your competitors) that can provide what the customer wants; to the "awareness set" of products the customer has heard of; to the "consideration set" of products the customer will evaluate further; to the "decision set," or the product the customer actually chooses.

Most marketers head straight for the decision set. They think their ads should be loaded with all the details that are going to push their customers past consideration and into the decision set.

But, as we've just mentioned, customers have a harder time believing a lot of claims. And unless you're doing direct marketing, your advertising isn't really trying to convince a prospect to buy on the spot anyway. All you want is consideration: talk to a sales rep, visit the dealer, look up the website, call this number, find out more. Mass media are ideal for messages that promote awareness and consideration. One study showed that people exposed to product ads were nearly twice as likely to buy those products as people not exposed to those ads.[2] And a 2004 study of technology purchases showed that 43.8 percent of decision-makers will strongly consider buying a product with high brand awareness, versus just 18.6 percent who would favorably consider buying a brand they've hardly heard of.[3]

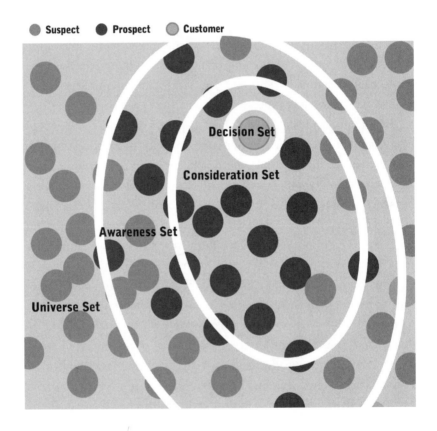

The customer mindset coninuum

In your customer's mind, all purchase decisions involve movement from the "universe set" of all products like yours, through the "awareness set" and "consideration set" to the actual purchase or "decision set." Moving from set to set requires a variety of strategies and considerations.

There's plenty of time to get complicated and cover all the details. That time is closer to the actual sale, and has more to do with "sales" than "marketing." If you want to really attract prospects, though, you have to keep the message simple and pointed. And you can't be afraid of the magic word.

And the Magic Word Is . . .

"No."

No, really. Perhaps the most important word in the marketer's dictionary is "no." In fact, one of the ways you can differentiate between sales and marketing is that sales is all about getting to "yes," whereas, in a profound way, marketing is about getting to "no."

What do I mean? Well, the idea of getting to "yes" is obvious. If you're a salesperson with a prospect on the line, you want to get your prospects nodding and keep them nodding until the sale has been consummated.

The same is true for marketing, of course. You want to find those prospects you can hand over to your salespeople who are going to nod all the way to the bank. But even more important, you have to get a lot of heads shaking "no." The reason, of course, is that the last thing you want to do is turn over bad prospects (wrong market segment) to your salespeople. Appealing to the wrong market segment does nothing but waste time, money, and effort. So good marketing efforts *must* be built around the idea of weeding out the chaff—that is, quickly and efficiently excluding people for whom your product is really not right. When you do this, you increase the appeal your offer has for the people you really do fit well.

I know this seems a little counterintuitive, but let's examine the idea for a moment. First, let's pretend you're a marketer for a company that makes optical scanners. You have a new scanner that's the world's fastest, bar none; in fact, it's three times faster than the next fastest machine on the market. You decide to build a marketing effort to generate leads, and lots of them. So you go out with a message that says, simply, "You have to experience this new scanner to believe it."

And you get a lot of leads; people *love* new things. But when you give the leads to your salespeople, here's what they find out:

- Lots of people don't care about the speed of your scanner. They're happy with a slow scanner.

- Some people wish their scanner worked faster, but image quality is more important to them and yours isn't good enough.

- Size is critical to some people. Some people have to fit the scanner in a crowded production line, and your scanner is quite a bit bigger than most.

- Some prospects care more about price than speed, image quality, or size.

- Other prospects care primarily about the dimensions of the image they can scan.

- A certain percentage of prospects cares about ease of repair, parts availability, and uptime versus downtime.

What's the percentage of leads you've invited into your marketing funnel and perhaps given to your salespeople that are simply no good? Even if it's only twenty or thirty percent—and it could be much, much more—you're wasting that much of your sales force's time. Instead of getting to "yes," they have to go through a lot of "no." And that's a job marketing can do far more efficiently.

Instead, what if you go out with a marketing message that says, "Scan Three Times Faster than Anything Else Available"? Here's what I think:

- You would drastically reduce the number of bad leads you turn over to your sales force. People who don't care about fast scanning won't waste their time responding.

- Your salespeople would close more sales quicker by being able to focus on legitimate prospects.

- The raw number of leads would probably go down, *but maybe not by much.* Remember, on one hand, general claims and lots of fuzzy bullet points don't attract attention, and on the other, invite skepticism. A more pointed approach could actually *increase* the raw number of leads—and they'd all be better qualified than the leads you'd get when appealing to everyone was your goal.

The point is this: when readers see your ad that says "Scan Three Times Faster than Anything Else Available," some of them say, "Yes, that's for me," and others say, "Nope, not interested." *And the "no" is at least as important as the "yes."* That's why smart marketers are never afraid of "no." They understand that "no" means their segmentation strategy is working beautifully. In fact, I maintain strategy is all about saying "no."

"Sure," you say, "but my product is different. My product is strong in a lot of areas. No one feature stands out. We have lots of strengths. We're not the best-quality product on the market, but we're right in there. Availability is pretty good. Service is in the top third of the industry." To go back to the scanner example, it's pretty fast, with a pretty good image, in a moderate size, at a decent price.

Well, I have some bad news for you.

Great Brands Get Bad Grades

Now that I've been all over the map with analogies in this chapter, I thought I'd add one more. This one, perhaps more than all the others, really brings home the key to this common mistake and what it means.

Great brands are, for the most part, D students.

Don't believe me? Think of a great brand. Let's consider one everyone knows: McDonald's.

McDonald's is not known for its high-caliber cuisine. You don't take the boss there on her birthday or your spouse there on your anniversary. The food at McDonald's is also far from the most healthful menu in town. **Food: D.**

Atmosphere isn't the chain's strong suit, either. It's not unpleasant, but it's not the sort of place you want to hang around all day; in fact, the colors and the hard seats and everything else about the place suggests it's an okay place to stop and gobble, but no place to linger over a cappuccino. **Atmosphere: D.**

Service? You've got to be kidding. Stand in line, grab your tray, and fill your own soft drink cup: **D.**

Fun? Ah, now we're getting somewhere.

Kids love McDonald's. McDonald's has built one of the world's great brands, in part, because of toys and playgrounds and food that appeals to kids.

And if you don't have kids, chances are good that you still eat at McDonald's because it's convenient and it's dependable. There's one on every corner and at every freeway exit, so it's easy to stop. And you may get a vastly superior hamburger at a local burger joint you've never heard of, but you might get a terrible hamburger, too. Why take chances when you know exactly what you're going to get at McDonald's?

So, yes, McDonald's does get at least one A. But it also gets a lot of Ds. And when you think about it, the problem with lots of other fast food chains is that they're B or C students, across the board.

It's that way with all sorts of products. You don't buy a Hummer for fuel efficiency. You don't buy an iPod because it will play your compact discs. You don't buy *Brand Busters* to read to the kids at bedtime.

Let's linger on iPods for one moment longer. The iPod has certainly been a hugely successful and much-imitated product. Even the models with the smallest hard drives can hold days' worth of music. Consumers can fit their entire music collections, and even their video libraries, on this tiny device. It's simply and elegantly designed. It has some versatility for storing other media—addresses and to-do lists and the like—but it's marketed and sold as a music and video player, and that's all most people use it for.

The iPod has been much imitated. As of this writing, all sorts of companies have media players on the market, some with technical advantages over the iPod—price, storage capacity, sound quality, functionality, you name it. But the iPod is still, by a wide margin, the industry leader because *it's a cool way to capture, store, and play your music and video.*

So why do you think *your* product should appeal to *everyone* in your category?

Here's a great exercise: make a list of all the factors that go into your prospects' buying decisions for your product. A representative list might include:

- Performance
- Price
- Service after the sale
- Availability
- Technical support
- Compatibility with other products

We'll stop there. Now, rate your product against all of these factors. Do you have one or two areas in which your product is outstanding? Or, to look at it from your customers' point of view, are there one or two reasons that come up repeatedly when you ask customers why they buy your product? Or, when you honestly evaluate your product, do you find yourself getting Bs across the board?

And now that you've done this exercise with your product, consider your competitors' products. How do they rate in the factors that are important to customers?

And one final note here: I'm not suggesting that you should not strive for excellence in all areas. McDonald's, for example, has done a lot to offer more healthful menu options and to eliminate some of its highest-fat-and-calorie options. Apple's iPod succeeds not only because of its single-focus simplicity, but also because of its sleek design, dependable technology, and the ease and simplicity of purchasing music and video at the iTunes website. I certainly don't think you should ignore the realities of price or delivery or any of the features your customers truly want and appreciate in products like yours. What I'm saying is that *your product doesn't have to be excellent in all areas for it to be successful* and claiming excellence in all areas only makes your marketing weak, unfocused, and difficult to believe.

That's my story, and I'm sticking to it. I suggest you find the story that works for you and do the same.

An Island You Can Command

What do the marketers we considered in the last section have in common? Clearly, McDonald's and Apple are market leaders. They dominate their markets in certain areas.

But not in all areas. As we've discussed, McDonald's isn't the place to go for a gourmet dinner. But they have created an island for themselves inside the sea of dining choices: the island of convenience and fun. It's their island, and no one touches them there.

Taking a closer look at Apple provides some additional perspective. I'll come back to the iPod in a moment. But first, let's look at Apple computers.

Apple has always been a strong brand with a highly developed sense of style and a fanatically loyal customer base. But it's not as if they haven't made mistakes. Back in the early days of personal computing, Apple held its products and its development code close to the vest. They didn't particularly want outside developers creating software for the Macintosh. They wanted control of their own destiny.

IBM, on the other hand, made its standards available to everyone. As a result, the PC exploded while the Macintosh puttered along. When it comes to personal computing, it's not really about the hardware, but about the software. And there was so much more software available for the PC—and so many people coming into the world of personal computing with so many different needs—that the PC became the more popular choice. It was also the lower-cost choice; dozens of hardware manufacturers began to knock out PCs, and the price kept going down.

Today, in virtually every industry, you'll find that the PC is the desktop computer of choice. In health care, manufacturing, insurance, banking, retailing—pick an industry, and the PC is king.

Oh, right: I said *virtually* every industry. Because Apple did manage to keep a stranglehold on a couple of them.

One is commercial design. Today in ad agencies, graphic design firms, photo studios, video professionals, and other visually creative endeavors, the Mac is ubiquitous. Most graphic designers have never worked on a PC. Most have no desire to.

Another is education. Although lots of schools do use PCs, lots of them use Macs, too. The Macintosh is still commonly thought of as the "user-friendly" option.

In general, Apple has cultivated a reputation as being the computing company for creative people. Fiction writers, screenwriters, artists, photographers, even scientists—all are more likely to use Macs than PCs.

In other words, even though the PC, through the use of open programming standards, became the personal computing choice of the masses, the Mac maintained an island it could command. Creative people tend to think of PCs as computers for "business." Macs are for people who, according to a long-running Apple campaign, "think different." And these are people who are proud of their differences. Clearly, Apple can command this island because it understands its audience very well. It said "no" to the masses, focusing instead on a couple of key market segments it could dominate. As a result, the company generated margins on its hardware that PC-makers could only dream of.

Now, think back to our discussion about the iPod. Does it do more than play music? Well, yes. Does it matter? Not today. The iPod is the simplest, coolest MP3 player out there. There's a whole continent of these small mass storage devices out there. "Media player" is the island Apple has chosen to command.

And—just to bring the point full circle—the majority of those songs I listed at the start of this chapter are available today at the iTunes website. Songs from the mid-70s are *still* making money for their creators. Some popular music artists from days gone by are still making millions of dollars a year in royalties because they found their audiences and pleased them. You can too, if you remember that your audience is *not* everybody.

What Should You Remember from Reading this Chapter?

- **In trying to appeal to everyone, marketers** weaken their message to the point that they **end up appealing to no one.**

- In marketing, it's about finding out the **strengths of your brand that really resonate with your customers** and making the most of them.

- Studies show **if you make a lot of claims in your ads, you're inviting greater skepticism** than if you make just one strong claim. Narrow your focus.

- Most marketers use mass media to try to get customers to make a decision about their product. **Mass media are ideal for creating awareness and consideration.** One study showed people exposed to product ads were nearly twice as likely to buy those products as people not exposed to those ads.

- One of the ways you can differentiate between sales and marketing is: **sales is all about getting to "yes,"** whereas in a profound way, **marketing is all about getting to "no."**

- **Your product doesn't have to be excellent in all areas** for it to be successful. Claiming excellence in all areas only makes your marketing weak, unfocused, and difficult to believe.

- **Great brands are, for the most part, D students.** Successful brands have found their audience and played to them. You can too if you remember your audience isn't everybody.

Brand Buster #5

Forgetting that People Forget

I'D LIKE TO BEGIN this chapter by revisiting my telescope story. You'll remember from the introduction how much trouble I had purchasing a telescope; as an amateur stargazer, I simply couldn't get past the scientific gobbledygook to determine which telescope might be right for me.

Eventually, with the help of a product review in *Sky & Telescope* magazine, I purchased a telescope from a company called Meade. Later, I came to understand that a different brand, Orion, positions itself as making the ideal telescopes for beginners. Going back to the idea I shared in the last chapter, you might say that "great telescopes for novice stargazers" is the island Orion can command.

But you'll also remember that, before I found the advice I needed in *Sky & Telescope,* I spent a long time devouring the ads. And when I recently thought back to those days, I didn't remember seeing any ads for Orion telescopes.

So I went back and looked again. To my surprise, Orion actually had three pages of ads in my old copy of *Sky & Telescope.*[1]

The problem is, one of Orion's competitors, Meade, had *10* pages of advertising in the magazine. I assumed at the time Meade was the market leader, and I've since learned that I was correct. As someone who at least *looked like* the market leader, they got my attention; that is, they quickly achieved *awareness* in the mind of this novice. Orion may have had the better product for me. But Meade had the better marketing strategy, and made the sale.

As a quick aside, I can't tell you how many times over the years I've heard smart marketers discount the fact that readers of trade and specialty magazines say they read these publications *specifically* for the advertisements. I purchased *Sky & Telescope* magazine, plain and simple, for the telescope ads. And I read all—yes, *all*—of them. And I still didn't remember ever seeing an ad for Orion.

Why? The answer is simple, really. One advertiser captured my attention with the value and selling power of *message frequency*. The other did not.

Back in my college days, I had a journalism professor who, without a trace of irony, informed the class that one of the cardinal rules of newspaper writing was, "Never repeat yourself. *Never* repeat yourself."

I'm here to tell you that one of the cardinal rules of marketing is, "Repeat yourself frequently." Without frequent repetition of your marketing messages, people forget about you. That's worth repeating: *without frequent repetition of your marketing messages, people forget about you.* And no prospect is going to buy your product unless they remember it as an option.

Remember the Ebbinghaus Curve?

Probably not. Hermann Ebbinghaus isn't a household name. If you had psychology or marketing classes in college, you may have encountered the Ebbinghaus Curve. But because it hasn't been on your radar screen in years, you've forgotten.

Allow me to refresh your memory. Hermann Ebbinghaus (1850-1909) was a German experimental psychologist who was one of the first to discover that learning and memory could be studied experimentally. Ebbinghaus used nonsense syllables in controlled experiments and plotted people's abilities to learn and forget them over time on a curve. It's become known as the Ebbinghaus Memory Retention Curve.

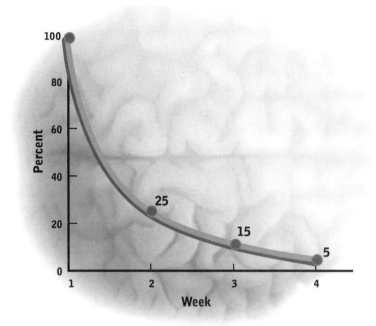

The curve of forgetfulness

Research shows that, without repeated exposure to new information learned, we remember only 25 percent of it after one week. After four weeks, we remember only 5 percent of the original information.

And it illustrates a truth that's as important as any you'll find in this book, and in practically any other book about marketing, for that matter.

Ebbinghaus found we forget 75 percent of new information we learn after seven days. After 30 days, we forget 95 percent of what we've learned.[2] So if you've ever wondered why you're hazy about the details of that news story you read a week ago—and can barely remember what you read a month ago—now you understand that it's normal.

So how do marketers combat forgetting? After all, customers aren't going to buy from you if they don't remember you.

One way to overcome forgetting is to use mnemonics: memorable creative devices that stick in your head. You no doubt remember television theme songs, commercial jingles, and advertising slogans from your youth. They were created for the express purpose of sticking in your head. As a matter of comparison, even though you might be able to whistle the theme song from *The Andy Griffith Show,* you almost certainly cannot recite the dialogue from your favorite episode. That's because the theme song has a pleasing and very memorable melody and the dialogue, while funny and engaging, doesn't have that sort of powerful hook.

But there's another reason you remember the theme song and not the dialogue: even if you've watched *The Andy Griffith Show* in reruns for decades, chances are good you've seen your favorite episode only a handful of times. But you've heard the theme song hundreds, maybe even thousands, of times.

Frequency is the key to building message awareness. And awareness has at least one very positive effect: it creates preference. Simply stated, people prefer things they're more familiar with. In one study, French researchers discovered the longer participants were exposed to random groups of black-and-white patterns, the more they liked them.[3] In another study, the more times people heard a particular musical score, the more positive they felt about the music.[4]

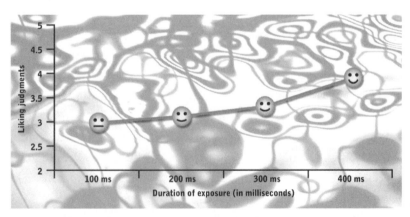

The longer you see something, the more you like it

Undergraduates at the University of Bourgogne in France were shown a random pattern of black-and-white shapes. Researchers reported the longer people were exposed to the pattern each time they saw it, the more they liked it.

The more you're exposed to something, the more you like it—and we've already discussed how important likeability is to your marketing. The question is, how much frequency does it take to make a message stick?

Hermann Ebbinghaus had some ideas about that, too. In another experiment, he discovered that it took 17 exposures to a bit of information for people to learn it.

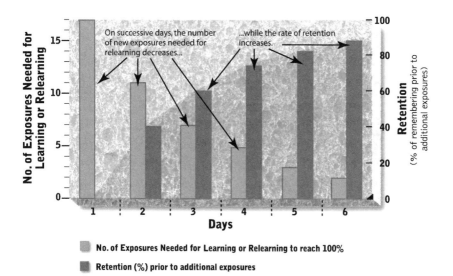

No. of Exposures Needed for Learning or Relearning to reach 100%
Retention (%) prior to additional exposures

The curve of retention

Ebbinghaus demonstrated that as exposure to information is repeated on successive days, the number of exposures needed to create memory decreases and the rate of retention increases.

The next day, he tested how much of the material his subjects remembered that they had supposedly learned—and found that they'd already forgotten 40 percent of it. Yet, with 11 exposures, he was able to boost their memories back up to 100 percent. The following day, it took eight exposures to completely restore the memories. The day after that, only five exposures were needed.[2]

The message here is that frequency is the key to remembering.

The more you are exposed to a message, the more likely you are to remember it.

This is an important message for all marketers. If you are doing, let's say, a print advertising campaign, it makes little or no sense to produce an ad that runs once (although some newer theories challenge this belief; more on this later). Lots of marketers who have used the same ad for a year think the ad is "tired." But the fact is, your audience is probably still just getting the message. Your tired ads probably aren't boring anybody but you. As a matter of fact, consider direct response advertisers whose ads appear mainly in the classified sections of magazines and newspapers. These advertisers often run the exact same ads for many years—decades, even. There's only one reason someone would run the same ad for decades: because it works.

So you run your ads and people become aware of you, and suddenly, they begin to prefer you, as well. Right? Well, yes and no.

Brand Awareness: The First Step Toward Brand Preference

Actually there's no "suddenly" about it. Marketing isn't magic. Building awareness is only a step on the road to preference.

Not too long ago, a couple of Penn State professors analyzed awareness and preference levels for more than a thousand products in the semiconductor industry.[5] What they found was the relationship between awareness and preference is not one-to-one; that is, just because 20 percent of the market is aware of your product doesn't mean 20 percent of the market prefers your product.

In reality, the relationship between brand awareness and preference follows an S-curve; that is, the relationship is logarithmic, not linear. What this means is that your brand must, at least initially, achieve fairly high levels of awareness to achieve even modest levels of preference

Successful companies with high brand awareness reach a point where additional dollars spent on awareness create roughly equivalent returns in terms of preference.

As awareness increases, brand preference increases more rapidly.

Initially, most companies must increase awareness significantly to achieve modest gains in brand preference.

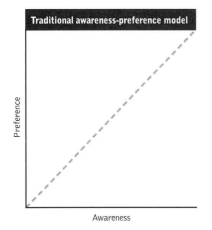

Traditional awareness-preference model

Preference

Awareness

Updated awareness-preference model

Preference

Successful companies

Most companies

Awareness

Conventional models assumed a 1:1 relationship between brand preferences and brand awareness.

The relationship between brand awareness and preference follows an S-shaped curve. Most companies must significantly increase awareness to achieve desired gains in brand preference.

Initially, your brand awareness has to reach 15 percent before buyer preference reaches a threshold share of two percent. If your brand has 30 percent awareness right now, you need a boost of four percent awareness to move the preference needle just one percent. You have to get to 70 percent awareness before preference reaches 25 percent.

But this is the point at which preference can really take off. In many cases, a boost in brand awareness to above 70 percent will yield a one-to-one boost in brand preference. And above 90 percent brand awareness gets you even more: one-and-a-quarter points in preference for every awareness point you raise.

Awareness advertising has long gotten a bad rap in the marketing industry. Marketers don't just want awareness: they want the prospect to *do* something. In days gone by, they wanted prospects to circle the number on the reader response card or make a trip to their grocer's and demand Sweetheart Soap. Today, the common desire is to "drive people to the web." Most marketers today *still* want people to take action as a result of seeing their advertisements.

And there's nothing wrong with that. Encouraging prospects to do something is a good thing. The big problem is that lots of marketers think their advertising is a sort of miracle drug; put it out there, and the customers will flock to your door. (Others, just as naïvely, believe advertising has no effect.)

There are a couple of things wrong with this thinking. The first is an idea we discussed in Chapter 3 (put forth by Rosser Reeves): your advertising can actually have a **negative** impact on your sales if people don't like it. The second is that some marketers think they shouldn't have to *do* anything else if the advertising is working. Again, unless your product lends itself to direct marketing, you shouldn't be expecting your ads to close sales.

What should you expect your ads to do? The fact is (as I mentioned in the previous chapter), targeted media advertising can build awareness and consideration. It helps move prospects from the Universe Set; to the Consideration Set to the Decision Set. That's the one you eventually want to be in, because it's the one in which the prospect becomes a customer.

Most marketers point their advertising directly toward the Decision Set. And why not? That's what you want, isn't it? Why not blow past those other rings and aim directly for the bullseye?

Because you can't get to the bullseye without going through the other rings. Perhaps instead of thinking of this idea as a set of concentric rings, we should imagine it as concentric spheres. You have to penetrate through Awareness and Consideration before you can reach the Decision Set. (Refer to the illustration on page 58.)

You may think this is hogwash. You may think you can get prospects to go directly from the Universe Set to the Decision Set. But I'd challenge you to think about this in your own consumer behavior. Here are a couple of examples:

You want to buy a telescope. You've never heard of Orion. By doing (too much!) research, you become aware of this company. You learn they make telescopes suitable for novices, so you decide it makes sense to consider them. You do a bit more investigating, and decide that an Orion is, indeed, the telescope for you. Universe to Awareness to Consideration to Purchase. Just like that—took about two months.

You're in the supermarket checkout line. You decide you want some gum. Your eye scans the candy rack. Orbit, Wrigley's Spearmint, Dentyne, Brite Wite. Huh. You've never heard of Brite Wite. You pick it up. It promises "fresher breath and a WITER smile!" You want fresh breath and a w(h)ite smile. It's wintergreen flavor. You love wintergreen. You're considering. It's seventy-five cents. You have seventy-five cents. Sold. Universe to Awareness to Consideration to Purchase. Just like that. Took about two seconds.

Here's the point: it doesn't matter whether it takes two months, two seconds, two minutes, or two years, for that matter. You *must* achieve awareness, however it happens, before you get customers to lay their money down. And media that target your audience can quickly and efficiently help you achieve awareness.

We've already talked a bit about how smart, appropriate creative work can help you gain awareness. But this chapter is about frequency. So I'm going to repeat the message: *people forget.* You have to achieve awareness to achieve sales. And you have to keep the message coming to ensure awareness. Otherwise, people will forget about you, and you'll have to start building awareness all over again.

How often do you have to send your message? We'll get to

that. But before we do, let's take a look at one more model of how customers go from "awareness" to "adoption"—a process that goes a littler further than the one we've explored above—and how it affects your marketing and sales efforts.

The Adoption Process: As Easy As AIETA

Marketers have studied customer behavior for decades. They've taken countless surveys, asked thousands of people tens of thousands of questions, poked, prodded, and read register receipts—all to find out how you get from finding out about a product to driving home with said product in your minivan. There's one widely accepted model of how it works called "AIETA," for reasons that will become obvious. According to this model, on their way to a purchase, prospects pass along the following continuum:[6]

1. **Awareness:** the prospect learns of the product, but knows little or nothing about it beyond its existence and some idea of its benefits.

2. **Interest:** the prospect becomes interested, seeks information, and begins to gather details.

3. **Evaluation:** the prospect imagines him- or herself using the product. At this point, the prospect asks the question, "Can I do it? Can I see myself as the owner of this product?"

4. **Trial:** the prospect experiments with the product on a small scale in an effort to become intimate with it and learn how to use it to his or her best advantage.

5. **Adoption:** the prospect begins large-scale use, which hopefully leads to preference, satisfaction, and repeat purchases.

The Adoption Model: AIETA

Depending on the product, these steps in the Adoption Model can progress rapidly or slowly. For technical and scientific products, the process is usually more drawn-out, involving weeks, months and sometimes even years of investigation and education.

Again, as with our sets model, these steps in the adoption process can occur rapidly or slowly. You can go from Step 1 to Step 4 in a matter of seconds with an impulse buy at the supermarket, and get to Step 5 after a couple of days of falling in love with a new brand of chewing gum. For other, more considered, purchases the process can involve weeks, months, and even years.

But here's the most interesting aspect of the AIETA model for our purposes: it provides clear direction for allocating resources between mass marketing and personal selling communications. In general, the closer to the beginning of the AIETA continuum your prospects are, the more cost effective mass communications will be. The nearer your prospects are to Adoption, the more personal selling comes into play.

As I've said, when you have a new or relatively unknown product, you must generate awareness. And mass media strategies—print advertising, broadcast advertising, trade shows, direct mail, web advertising—are often ideal for raising awareness. That's because they allow you to reach the most people for the least cost per exposure. (Actually, direct mail has a relatively high cost per exposure, sometimes measured as "cost per thousand" or CPM. Because you have to produce a printed piece and mail it, it's relatively expensive. Postage alone will cost you hundreds of dollars per thousand—compared with a CPM of pennies for some forms of mass advertising. But direct mail has at least two more advantages that make it worth considering for many marketers: it allows pinpoint targeting of prospects, and it communicates one-to-one, as opposed to, for example, print or web ads that have to compete with all the other ads.)

Mass media reach a mass audience. Lots of people get exposed to your message. When they've been exposed a number of times, you achieve awareness and perhaps begin to generate interest in your product, which, you hope, prompts evaluation. Ads, websites, product literature, and other informative and persuasive communications can help you provide prospects with the knowledge they need to move further along the adoption continuum.

And here is where personal selling begins to have a more significant role in the process of making a sale. Personal selling can get that persuasive, informative material into prospects' hands and get them moving toward trial. Particularly for large-ticket items and technical and scientific products, personal selling can be critical. After you've achieved awareness and interest and have encouraged evaluation, mass communications become less effective for the job at hand, since your prospects need more information than you can easily or logically communicate in an ad or television spot. You need sales tools and salespeople to answer questions and help prospects decide how best to use your products.

Salespeople and customer service personnel can be even more instrumental in helping customers move from trial to adoption. Good customer service can actually be the element that tips the scale in favor of large-scale use. To go back to the now-familiar story: my reading got me thinking about Meade telescopes, generated interest, and led to evaluation. But brochures and spec sheets—that is, sales materials—and a helpful salesperson were needed to provide enough information to close the sale.

So where do *your* prospects fall along the AIETA continuum? Or, to mix models for a moment, are they all still out there in the Universe Set, waiting to hear about you?

Chances are, unless you have a brand-new product, you'll find prospects all along the continuum. Some are aware, but not yet interested. Some are interested, but not so interested they're ready to evaluate your product. Some are doing due diligence, and not yet ready to pull the trigger on trial. Some are trying, and not quite ready to commit to adoption. What this means (certainly if you are marketing a large, expensive, technical, or scientific product) is that you need both sales and marketing, and you need to consider where most of your prospects lie along the continuum to make the most effective use of your marketing dollars. But you can't just drop one end of the spectrum in favor of the others. You need mass media **and** personal selling.

One more point before we move on. Many marketing gurus have

been noting for years that mass media are in decline. Huge advertisers, such as McDonald's, are spending a substantially smaller percentage of their advertising budgets on traditional mass media. But the key to understanding this trend is the word "traditional." Advertisers are finding *new ways to reach the masses:* web advertising, mobile, email, in-mall advertising, movie and television placements, and other strategies. Some retailers have created their own in-store networks where brands they carry can advertise, allowing them to place persuasive commercial messages much closer to the point of purchase.

This book is about marketing, not advertising, per se. I'm not going to get into a debate about the best media for reaching your prospects. The point remains that the more you need awareness and consideration (or interest and evaluation), the more you need the mass media—whatever that means in your product category—to reach your target cost effectively.

How Little Is Too Little? How Much Is Too Much?

How much advertising? The debate has been with us since Neanderthals scrawled out those very first cave paintings. "How many of these suckers do I have to paint before the rest of the gang gets the idea that to eat, we gotta hunt?" You get the picture.

Today, the answer pretty much comes down to two theories: frequency and recency.

The traditional (frequency) theory says, for the most part: the more frequency, the better (up to a point). Along these lines, here's the rule of thumb that has dominated the discussion: People need to be exposed to a message between 3 and 11 times before they remember it.[7] The "frequency" theory places a lot of stock in the psychology of memory and learning. (I'm only skimming the surface here. For an in-depth look at frequency research, I suggest you read Colin McDonald's *Advertising Reach and Frequency,* 2nd edition, 1996.[8])

Using the "frequency" theory, advertisers who can't afford to continuously sustain a 3-to-11 exposure threshold bunch their advertising into "flights." For several weeks or months at a time, they run these flights of advertising at heavy (3 to 11) frequency. Then they drop out for a few weeks or months at a time.

The other major theory began in the early 1990s, introduced by John Philip Jones in his book *When Ads Work*.[9] This theory takes a much different approach. It says one exposure is often enough to do the trick. Jones (and now others, including McDonald) believes advertising should "be there" right before a person makes a purchase decision. And since we never quite know exactly when any specific person will make that decision, we need to be in front of our audience all the time, or as continuously as our resources allow. The theory states that advertising messages work mostly with the small number of people who happen to be "in the market" at the moment they are exposed to the message. Think of it as presence. "*When* is more important than *how many*," says media planning guru Erwin Ephron.[10] A single exposure (albeit perhaps not the first exposure) can trigger a purchase. Believers in this theory call it the "recency" approach. (As in how *recently*, prior to the purchase decision, has the person been exposed to the message?)

I find the recency theory makes a lot of sense to my technical and scientific clients. They relate to the idea of their salesperson being the last one the buyer sees before he decides which brand to purchase. This sums up the recency theory quite nicely.

According to the Recency Theory, only one exposure—the most recent—may prompt those already in the buying mode to purchase your product. Continuous (albeit lower level) exposure sums up this approach. The "frequency" model favors higher levels—even if it means dropping out of the media from time to time.

Here's a simple example. Rather than advertising in each of his market's four main trade publications every other month, the "recency" devotée runs an ad in two pubs every month. Why? He believes buyers continuously make purchase decisions (and not just every other month). A caution from Mr. Obvious: don't use this thinking for seasonal products like snow shovels.

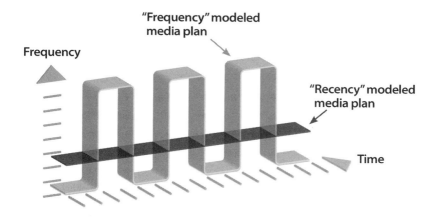

Frequency vs. Recency Model

Marketers who employ the "recency" approach stretch their advertising exposures. Their goal is for messages to appear continuously in front of the most people.

So which theory should you use? Frequency? Or recency?

Practically speaking, the recency theory places more emphasis on reach (the number of people who have an opportunity to see your advertising). The theory goes that It's better for your message to appear before 30,000 people one time than it is to appear before 10,000 people three times. It also emphasizes when versus how many. According to Erwin Ephron, "The evidence shows reaching three consumers once will result in more sales than repeatedly reaching one consumer—and the costs are the same."[10]

Frequency theory says exposing a person to your message less than three times is wasteful. It encourages marketers to restrict reach in favor of frequency (it's better to reach 10,000 people three times than to reach 30,000 people one time).

If you follow this sort of thing, the recency theory seems to be the prevailing thinking of today. Yet, generally speaking, the net effect of either theory is that you should be in front of your audience with regularity. When it comes right down to it, both approaches say you need more than just limited exposure to achieve results.

And neither theory would have you run just one ad and expect much to happen.

The bottom line? I'm not so sure it matters much which theory you rely on. Depending on your situation, one theory or the other may make more sense to you intuitively. I say go with that. Either theory will have you considering the best ways to get your message into the marketplace multiple times for maximum effect.

Finally, before we leave our discussion of memory and how much advertising is enough, please understand my comments are general in nature. They only scratch the surface of the body of knowledge out there on this fascinating and ever-changing topic.

Also know that most of what is known about advertising effects on memory, ad-liking, frequency, and recency come from the world of consumer packaged goods (cereal, soap, perfume, and the like). Why is that? Because business-to-business markets simply aren't big enough to warrant the expenditures it takes to figure this stuff out. The annual budget for most marketers of a technical or scientific product wouldn't begin to fund even one sophisticated study like the ones I've discussed in this chapter.

So, we technical/scientific folks must make do with the next best thing—mountains of advertising research from the world of consumer goods. Is it perfect for our application? No. Is it better than nothing? Without question. And can it give us valuable clues on how to best direct our marketing efforts? You bet. We'd be fools not to take advantage of it.

What Should You Remember from Reading this Chapter?

- ☞ **Repeat yourself frequently.** Without frequent repetition of your marketing messages, people forget about you.

- ☞ Studies show **after 30 days, we forget 95 percent** of what we've learned.

☞ **People prefer things they're familiar with.** French researchers discovered the longer participants were exposed to random groups of black-and-white patterns, the more they liked them.

☞ **Building awareness is only a step on the road to preference.** Studies show your brand must, at least initially, achieve fairly high levels of awareness to achieve even modest levels of preference.

☞ Targeted media advertising can build awareness and consideration. **Marketers need to penetrate through awareness and consideration before they can reach the prospect's Decision set.**

☞ **The AIETA Model suggests on their way to a purchase, prospects pass through a 5-step continuum**. These steps can progress rapidly or slowly.

☞ **Marketers who employ the "recency" approach stretch their advertising exposures.** The goal is for messages to appear continuously in front of the most people.

☞ Frequency theory says **exposing a person to your message less than three times is wasteful**.

Brand Buster #6

Believing Your Price Is Too High— Without Proof

IF YOU DO ANY TRAVELING AT ALL—or even if you just watch the news—you're almost certainly familiar with the woes of the airline industry, especially since September 11, 2001. Again and again, airlines have failed, merged, and cut service, much to the chagrin of air travelers across the nation and around the world. The situation has definitely made air travel more difficult and less dependable.

It's easy to blame problems in the airline industry on the events of 9/11. But the U.S. airline industry's financial problems can be traced to something that started nearly a decade earlier—the great airline price war of 1992. Carriers began slashing fares, and every other carrier had to beat or match those fares to compete, which led to more and more price cutting.

Did it work? It depends upon how you measure success. Air travel rose to record levels. More people were flying than ever before. Flights were full. Travelers saved money.

And the airlines posted record financial losses. According to the *Harvard Business Review*, "Some estimates suggest that the overall losses suffered by the industry that year exceed the combined profits for the entire industry from its inception."[1]

I would rank that as a failure of colossal proportions. The airline industry hemorrhaged money. And a weak, financially strapped industry simply cannot weather times when other events—such as 9/11—cause a sharp decline in demand. Ultimately, you can't "make it up in volume." Losing money is losing money, period.

So why, time and again, is cutting price the strategy of first resort when sales are sluggish? And who says people make purchase decisions based on price anyway?

For the most part, they don't. Price is usually a consideration, but it's far from the most important factor in most purchase decisions, especially business-to-business purchase decisions. Unless you make the price so low that people can't help but buy, as in the example of the airline price war.

The big question is, what are you losing when you cut price without trying other strategies for gaining a competitive advantage?

The first thing you can lose is the trust and respect of your customers. I can say for myself that every time I see a retailer advertising "new lower prices," my first thought is, "Hmm. I wonder how much they were ripping me off before?" It's not an outlandish or insignificant question. If you can afford to sell me candy bars for fifty cents today, I'm not happy at all that I've been paying a dollar for them for the past two years. I wonder, "Did you finally get caught taking advantage of people?"

And that's just one of the consequences of believing your price is too high—without proof. (Yes, I'm willing to grant that maybe, in fact, your price *is* too high. But do you have proof?) I think you'll find some of the other consequences surprising—if not downright shocking. Read on.

Why Is Your Knee Jerking Like That?

It's quite common, really, this urge to lower your price. An article in the November 2006 issue of the *Harvard Business Review* "guesstimated" the average "negotiated discount" on business software at 25 percent—with discounts often exceeding 50 percent.[2] Cutting price is an easy place to begin if people aren't buying your product. It appeals to the all-American sense of "bargains"; if it isn't selling, maybe it just isn't cheap enough. And it's true: we all like to think we're getting a "deal" when we go out to market. That's why, for example, car buyers continue to put up with the antiquated practice of "bargaining" with their car dealers—and why dealers continue to advertise stripped-down vehicles most customers are never going to actually buy.

But just to stick with automobiles for a moment, do people *really* buy on price? If they did, everyone would buy a Yugo—that is, if Yugos were still being sold in the U.S., which they have not been since the early 1990s, because nobody was interested in buying them. Nor are the least expensive new cars available in the U.S. the best-selling cars in the U.S. today. At least when it comes to cars, people don't buy strictly on price.

Here's another example that's probably not original with me, but it's shocking and illustrative, nonetheless. Not long ago, my wife Sally and I were out for a drive when I noticed I needed gasoline. We pulled up in front of the gas pump. I filled the tank while Sally went into the convenience store. She came back with a bottle of water.

As we were pulling away, Sally glanced at the gas pump. "Fifty dollars to fill up your car?" she exclaimed. "That's ridiculous." And at first blush, I agreed. Gas had climbed to nearly three dollars a gallon, and fifty dollars was far more than I'd been used to paying just a few months previously.

But then I took a look at the bottle of water in Sally's hand. (I've always been a bit irritated by the whole idea of paying for a bottle of water. I'm sure it's played havoc with the drinking fountain industry.)

Anyway, I couldn't help but goad Sally. "You think gas is expensive?" I asked, "What do you think it would cost us to fill the gas tank with bottled water?" Neither one of us could do the math in the car, but I couldn't stop thinking about it. So later that evening, I pulled out my calculator. The answer might surprise you. It sure surprised me.

To fill my tank with gas that afternoon, I paid $53.57. That seems like a lot of money, doesn't it? To fill my tank with the brand of bottled water Sally bought would have cost me $161.14.

If it cost $161.14 to fill my tank with gasoline, there'd be a

Congressional investigation, but sales of bottled water continue to rise. This, remember, for a commodity you can still get free for the asking in most restaurants and public places.

I know, I know. Comparing water and gasoline is like comparing apples and dump trucks. But the point is, we're outraged by the price of the fuel that runs the engines of industry here and around the world; yet, we don't think twice about paying many times the same price for something we've been used to thinking of as "free."

But let's go ahead and make the apples-and-apples comparison because I don't have to buy bottled water. I can buy all my water from the low-cost supplier in my town, which happens to be India-napolis Water (IW). For that same $161.14 it would cost to fill my gas tank with bottled water, I could buy 92,965 gallons of water from IW. (They deliver right to my home, as well, at no additional charge.) Or, if I wanted to spend only the $1.09 I spent on bottled water, I could get 629 gallons from the water company.

So, where does that leave us? Gasoline: somewhere over three dollars a gallon at this writing. Bottled water: $6.98 a gallon. Tap water: $0.0017 a gallon. And yet, Sally plunked down the money to buy the bottled water without thinking twice about it. And if I know Sally—and I do—she'll do it again tomorrow.

The next time you start to believe that people buy on price, remember that millions of people are paying 4,027 times more than they need to for water. Can you imagine having a competitor charging 4,027 times more than you for a similar product? And winning? No wonder the drinking fountain industry is in the toilet.

A Few High-Priced Benefits

The message is clear: price is just one factor in the marketing mix. If price were the most important factor in the buying decision, low price would always win. Clearly, it does not. You don't have to have the low price to sell a lot of products.

Or services. I don't mind saying that I pay a lot more per hour for my law firm's services than I would pay for using LegalZoom online. Why will I pay more to listen to my attorney Vicki's advice? Because her advice is worth more, so it's a better value. You'll also pay more for tickets to see Bruce Springsteen than you'll pay for the Joe Average Band. You know, with Springsteen, that you're going to get an amazing show.

You'll pay more for a Mercedes than a Kia. More for a Sub Zero refrigerator than a Kenmore. More for a ring from Tiffany than one from Diamonds-R-Us.

Low Price	High Price
Advantages • Easy to communicate • Drives focused brand position • Will always appeal to a segment of the market (segment size can be small or large depending on category) **Potential Risks** • Connotes high risk, low quality, because people expect what they pay for • Hard to credibly own marketing "power positions" of reliability, quality, innovation, etc. • Creates a low cost mentality internally and externally • Won't eliminate price objections; some customers will always want a cheaper option • Focuses on low cost instead of best results or highest value • Only one company can be the low-price winner	**Advantages** • In most cases, suggests high value • May increase perceived brand value over the competition • Drives company profits • Allows for investments in quality, R&D, etc. to promote product pipeline and future innovations • Enables high levels of marketing and advertising to improve frequency and continuity of brand messages • Attracts the right audience: buyers who seek value, rather than those who shop based only on price • Often attracts a more brand-loyal audience **Potential Risks** • Eliminates potential audience segment who buys based on price • Adds pressure on marketing to demonstrate value that justifies price

Low vs. high brand price

How you price your product gives you rights to specific advantages and risks.

In most cases, high price suggests high value. Customers expect to get more with a high-priced product—and, in many cases, "more" is exactly what they're looking for. If the Mercedes/Yugo comparison seems a little extreme, consider that for many years American car buyers have bought Toyota and Honda products that were priced higher than the American competition because of superior performance and reliability and this in the face of substantial pressure to "buy American."

High price suggests value not only to your customers, but also throughout your organization and even your supply chain. When you have a high-priced product, your entire organization begins to adopt a high-value culture, exactly what you need when you've decided not to compete on price.

High price is also the engine that drives profits as we'll discuss in more detail a little later in this chapter. For now, the point is that high profits allow you to invest in improvements across the board—better technology, better personnel, improvements in the quality of your products, better market research, more advertising and marketing to drive more sales, and on and on.

High price also helps you attract the right kinds of happy customers. Remember how, in Chapter 4, we talked about "no" being the magic word in marketing? Well, high price helps you get to "no" pretty quickly. A high price tag eliminates prospects who buy on price, leaving you with buyers who are more concerned with benefits and value. These buyers also tend to be more brand loyal; they won't switch brands every time a lower-priced product comes along.

High price suggests high value and attracts value- and benefit-driven buyers. High price helps build a value-driven organization. High price drives high profits, which can help you drive better quality, employee satisfaction, and happy customers. And studies show that happy employees help you create happy customers. So why lower your price?

To be fair, being the low-price product has its advantages, too. For one thing, "We're the low-price leader" is a clear and focused market position to own. It's also easy to communicate. You don't have to get too fancy to get your point across. And low price certainly does appeal to a certain kind of buyer.

But low price also has a number of disadvantages. A big one is that low price makes it difficult, if not impossible, for you to own the marketing power positions: reliability, performance, and innovation. One thing most people believe is that "you get what you pay for." Know why they believe it? Because it's true. Most of the time, you pay more for better products because they're worth more. So if you own the low-price position, prospects have trouble believing you can deliver a product that measures up to the competition.

Low price can be poison for your organization. It engenders a corporate culture that's focused on driving down costs and cutting things out. These organizations operate more from a scarcity mentality rather than one that focuses on embellishing product value, boosting customer service, and so on. The mantra becomes, "find a cheaper way" instead of "find a better way." Have you ever worked for one of these companies? How long did you stay? Just as important, did you have lots of customers who were rabid fans of your company and your product?

Now, in all fairness, some companies succeed with a low-cost strategy. And they have their share of rabid fans. But, the fact is, there can be only one winner per category in the low-cost sweepstakes. There's only one Wal-Mart. Much to the chagrin of Kmart, Sears, JCPenney, Woolworth's, and other less-aggressive low-price competitors, some of them gone from the corporate landscape forever. You live by low price, and you can die by low price.

Finally, and most insidiously, low price will not eliminate price objections. No matter how low your price, some buyers will always want and even expect you to sell your product cheaper. My own experience as a marketer of services makes the point very well. When prospects call me today, they either already know or soon find out that I'm expensive. They rarely ask for a discount, and won't get one if they do. You see, I learned long ago that, to offer a discount, I needed to cut things out. The "product" I offered then suffered. And when the product suffered, my clients didn't get their problems solved. (Not to mention the fact that what I was offering started to look eerily similar to what my competitors were offering.) My clients are willing to pay more to work with me, because they understand my advice is worth the cost. Should it ever stop providing that value, they'll go somewhere else. And they should. That's the beauty of the free enterprise system.

So here's the question: would you rather attract customers who are constantly looking for a bargain? Or customers who appreciate your talents and are willing to pay for them? I can tell you firsthand that by raising my price, I actually attracted better clients—and got rid of the ones who always wanted a deal and forced me into producing a bad product. I was also able to plow my profits back into the business and continually upgrade the level of service and talent I could provide. Things had a way of spiraling up instead of down, as with airline ticket prices.

In summary, a higher price can help you attract and keep better customers. High price helps you get to "no" faster and weed out customers you don't want. High price says something more positive than words about the quality and value of your product. High price can drive higher profits, which helps you build a better organization.

And cutting your price even a little bit can have a dramatic impact on those profits. How dramatic? If I still haven't quite convinced you that you ought to think long and hard before you cut your prices, this next section could be the one that keeps you up at night.

Let's Look at the Numbers

You're no doubt familiar with the idea of "making it up on volume"; that is, lowering the price of your product to a bargain-basement level so that everyone buys it and you sell so many you can't help but make lots of money.

Great in theory, I suppose, although to me, it also sounds like a lot more work. You're sacrificing margin in an attempt to gain volume. So to make up what you're losing in volume, you just have to sell a little bit more. Right?

Don't answer yet.

Let's say your widget sells a million units at a dollar each. Cost of production is 60 cents, which means you're making a 40 percent margin on every widget you sell.

Then you find out Consolidated Widget is undercutting your price by 10 percent. In response, you decide to cut price 20 percent; after all, you have margin you can play with. Effectively, you decide to cut your margin in half. Hurray! You're sure to sell loads more widgets!

You'd better. In fact, you have to sell *double* the number of widgets to make the same amount of money.

It's simple mathematics. Cut the margin in half, and you have to achieve double the sales volume just to stay where you were—even though you only cut your price by 20 percent. If you're really lucky, you'll sell so many widgets that you'll corner the widget market, but at what cost to your workers and your production processes? And what about the wear and tear on your equipment? And the drag on capital investment needed to keep pace with demand? And what if that kind of volume increase just doesn't exist?

Or look at the problem this way: if you could find a way to sell only one more widget at your old price, you'd make more money than you would selling a million more widgets at your new price.

This example is obviously a dramatic oversimplification of the effect of lowering prices. But the numbers are real. And the fact that it's an overly simple example shouldn't undercut the truth: even a small reduction in price can have a huge negative multiplier effect on your margin and, thus, your profitability. So cut your prices if you must. Just do the math before you start slashing.

And, just maybe, there are a few other things you ought to try before you cut price.

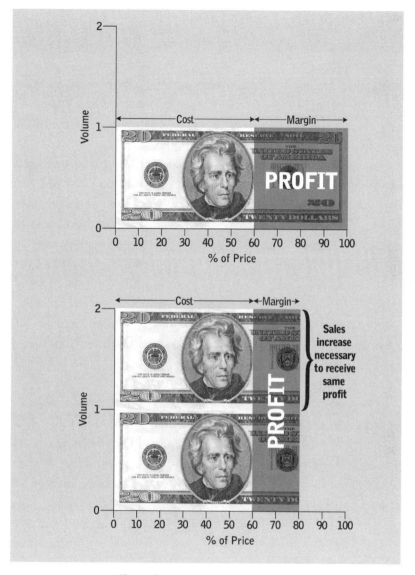

Effect of price on required volume

For a product with a 60 percent cost and a 40 percent margin, a 20 percent price reduction cuts margin in half. For a product selling one million units, sales must double to make up for the lost margin and maintain profit. (Adapted from *Power Pricing*, Dolan and Simon, 1996)

What Else to Try

First, try a different mindset. In most cases, you're safe in assuming your price probably isn't too high. Remember: people will pay a higher price for a product they prefer. And think about what you're giving up in the minds of your customers when you lower your price. You may lose prestige and trust, which can certainly lead to lost sales.

In my experience, most price objections are really questions about value received. A "price objector" is in a sense telling you that what he's paying and what he's getting aren't in balance. So why not focus on the real problem? To do that, you need to work on better communicating how your product gives your buyers what they want.

That's another side of the same coin: turning features into benefits and benefits into things people really *want*. We give this idea lots of lip service in my industry, but it's still a challenge to change your thinking and think in terms of offering customers fulfillment rather than features. (Now may be a good time to go back and review Chapter 2.)

Think "addition" rather than "subtraction." What have you added—or what can you add—to your brand to make it more valuable in the eyes of your customers and prospects? Or what can you add to your communications to remind customers that your brand already *is* more valuable? A change in message may be all that's required.

And when in doubt about whether your price is too high, ask. People will tell you whether or not they're willing to pay your price for your product.

But don't ask your salespeople. At least, be skeptical of "salesperson research." Salespeople are charged with selling, and they generally believe lower prices will help them sell more product. Their answers to the high-price question should never be considered reliable.

Instead, ask your customers. Here's how.

With A Name Like "The van Westendorp Technique," It's Gotta Be Good

Is it really a good idea to ask your customers what price they should pay for your product? Won't they just "lowball" you in an effort to save money? And if you take their advice and just happen to sell more, who's to say you can do it at a profit? All good points, I assure you, points that underscore the perils of pricing research. So what's a marketer to do?

Enter the van Westendorp technique (also called the Price Sensitivity Meter), a fairly simple method developed in the 1970s by Dutch economist Peter van Westendorp.[3] The premise behind the technique is that consumers can't tell you the "perfect" price to charge for your product. But they can give you a variety of opinions around the reasonableness of a price—clues—that when combined, establish boundaries around which to set price. The technique yields a price consumers are "willing to pay."

Survey participants are given a detailed description of the product (and/or mock-ups, photos, brand names, even a sample, face-to-face, if feasible) and then asked four questions:

1. At what price would you consider this to be a bargain—a great buy for the money? (Cheap)

2. At what price would it start to get expensive—still worth considering—but you'd have to give some thought before buying it? (Expensive)

3. At what price would it be so expensive that you wouldn't consider it at all? (Too expensive)

4. At what price would you consider the price to be so low that you'd begin to doubt the quality? (Too cheap)

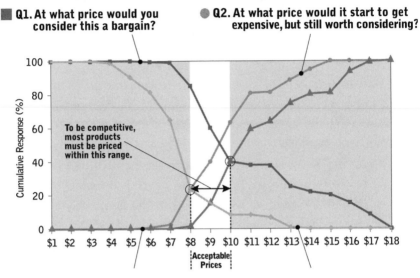

Q1. At what price would you consider this a bargain?

Q2. At what price would it start to get expensive, but still worth considering?

To be competitive, most products must be priced within this range.

Acceptable Prices

Q3. At what price would it be too expensive to consider?

Q4. At what price would it be so cheap you'd doubt its quality?

Van Westendorp price sensitivity meter

Plotting responses to price-sensitivity questions identifies a range of prices acceptable to your market ($8 to $10 in this example, but it doesn't show purchase intent. You'll still have to consider variables such as margin, costs and business objectives to zero in on the right price for your situation.

Once the responses are gathered, data are plotted on a graph—one line for each of the four questions (cheap, expensive, too cheap, too expensive). Take a look at the graph and you'll see four points at which the lines intersect. These points represent a price at which:

- the number of people who believe the price is a bargain (Q.1) equals the number of people who believe it is starting to get expensive (Q.2). Van Westendorp called this the Indifference Price Point (IPP).

- the number of people who reject the product as too cheap

(Q.4) equals the number of people who reject it as too expensive (Q.3). This is called the Optimum Price Point (OPP).

- the number of people who believe the product is starting to get expensive (Q.2) equals the number of people who reject for being too cheap (Q.4). This is called the Point of Marginal Cheapness (PMC).

- the number of people who consider the product a bargain (Q.1) equals the number of people who reject it as too expensive (Q.3). This is called the Point of Marginal Expensiveness (PME).

As you can see from the graphic, the intersection points give you boundaries. They don't give you a single answer and that's how I think you should look at this. There really is no single, perfect answer to the question of price. In fact, let's say you conduct a van Westendorp test—you'd still need to incorporate other details into your pricing decision. You'd need to consider cost of manufacturing, competitor pricing, revenue goals, and perhaps many other facts.

In summary, the van Westendorp method is by no means the perfect way to set price (nor is any other single method). In fact, some pricing experts would argue that consumer behavior is superior to opinion. (In other words: what does the consumer *do* vs. what does he *say* he will do.) So test markets have favor with these folks. But is it better than intuition or a poll of your salespeople? I believe it is. So think of it as something you can use, along with your own judgment, to help make a better pricing decision.

Finally, please know there are many ways of conducting pricing research—some quite sophisticated. I like van Westendorp because it's "do-it-yourself" simple. For lots more information on additional pricing methods and research, check out the Professional Pricing Society, of which I'm a former member, at *www.pricingsociety. com.*

And yes, sometimes it is appropriate to lower your price. But you need to be aware of what you're giving up when you do: profit margin, the appearance of quality, and maybe the trust of consumers who've been paying a higher price for the same product.

Here's an example you can probably relate to: at this writing, the housing industry in America is in a funk. (When you read this, the market may have flip-flopped. But the point still stands.) Lots of new homebuilders, nervous about their stockholders and all their unsold homes, are selling them at prices $40,000 to $80,000 lower than just a few months ago.

To be clear: today, I can buy a new house for $80,000 *less* than the guy next door paid last spring? This may seem like a good deal for me, but is it? My neighbor doesn't think so. His property value has just plummeted. Seems as if, all of a sudden, my new house is on shaky ground, too.

Life During (Price) Wartime

So you've taken everything into consideration. You've run the numbers, adjusted your messaging, asked your customers about your pricing. And in spite of your market savvy and your best intentions, you find yourself in a bona fide price war. What do you do now?

Here's a case study to ponder: the story of how 3M Corporation dealt with this issue of price pressure against their Post-It brand of sticky notes.

For years, Post-It was the premier brand—in fact, it was the only brand—in the category. "Post-It" became the generic term for sticky notes.

Inevitably, 3M began to face low-price competition. In fact, when I look online at the prices for sticky notes, I can find a pack of twelve 1" x 2" Post-It Notes brand selling for $7.20, while the competition—Highland—sells the same size 12-pack for $3.33, less than half the price for a product that does just about the same thing. How in the world can 3M compete with that?

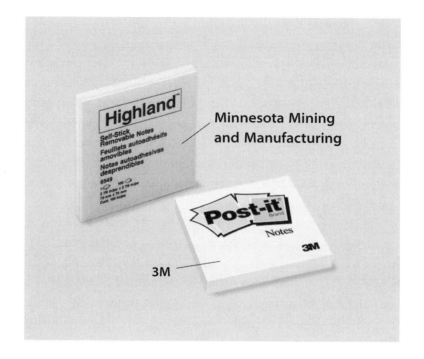

3M vs. Minnesota Mining and Manufacturing

3M uses distinct brands to appeal to premium and low-price markets.

It doesn't. Look closely at a packet of Highland Notes, and you'll see they're manufactured by a company called "Minnesota Mining and Manufacturing." We know this company better as 3M.

Rather than lower the price of Post-It Notes and erode its image and margin, 3M launched what's known as a "fighting brand"—a second product priced lower and designed especially to take category profits from low-price competition. You'll notice when you look at the packages side-by-side that you don't get the same appearance of quality with Highland as with Post-It. Highland's packaging is somewhat downscale and generic (plain type, one-color printing). And the color of the notes is washed out compared with the vibrant color you get with Post-It Notes. The message is clear: Post-It costs more and looks like it should. Highland looks cheap because it is cheap.

Marketers launch fighting brands all the time. Beer companies have premium-priced beer and value-priced beer. Canneries put green beans in one can and slap on a brand-name label—then put the same beans in another can and slap on a generic label. Establishing a fighting brand can be an effective, aggressive way of countering price competition without destroying your brand or your profit margin. Is this a way for you to fight a price war without your premium brand getting bloodied?

One more thing to consider about price. How about raising it?

An exercise I often use with my clients is to ask this question: "What would we need to do to be able to raise our price 10 percent? Twenty percent?" The answers I get back often revolve around such things as better communicating our current value, offering more data or information or ways customers can get increased performance, improvements in packaging (size, ease of use, etc.), enhancements in technical support—the list usually goes on and on.

In some cases, my clients have gained the ideas and courage they need to embellish their offerings and go for a price increase. In other cases, they've discovered some new concepts to incorporate into their value message and gained the fortitude to stave off those forces urging them to cut price. Either way, my clients and their customers have ended up better off. Try my exercise next time you face an angry internal mob demanding price cuts.

And finally, speaking of price increases, what do the data say? Eric Marder, in his excellent book *The Laws of Choice: Predicting Customer Behavior*, recounts what he learned over his many decades investigating how markets behave in response to price increases. [4] He calls it "the Price Effect Principle," and it goes like this:

"On average, a price increase of 10 percent will produce a share decrease of around nine percent, but there is a great deal of variability in this result. One time in five, the loss will be much larger, and one time in five there will be no loss at all."

More food for thought—and just one more thing you should consider before believing your price is too high.

What Should You Remember from Reading this Chapter?

- ☞ **Price is usually a consideration, but it's far from the most important factor** in most purchase decisions, especially in business-to-business purchase decisions.

- ☞ **In most cases, high price suggests high value.** Customers expect to get more with a high-priced product. A higher price can help you attract and keep better customers.

- ☞ **High price also drives high profits**, which can help you drive better quality, employee satisfaction and happy customers.

- ☞ The low price product has its advantages too. **"We're the low-price leader" is a clear and focused market position to own.**

- ☞ Low price also has a number of disadvantages. **A low price makes it difficult, if not impossible, for you to own the marketing power positions:** reliability, performance, and innovation.

- ☞ **Low price will not eliminate price objections.** No matter how low your price, some buyer will always want and even expect you to sell your products cheaper.

- ☞ Before you cut your price, there are a few other things to try. **Try a different mindset. You're safe in assuming your price probably isn't too high.**

- ☞ Most price objections are really questions about value received. **Work on better communicating how your product gives your buyers what they want.**

- ☞ **Establishing a fighting brand** can be an effective, aggressive way of countering price competition without destroying your brand or your profit margin.

# Brand Buster #7

Believing You Must Sell Your Product on an Economic Basis

WE'VE JUST SPENT an entire chapter talking about the inadvisability of cutting price. Time and time again, we see that low price is not the most important consideration in purchase decisions, especially for technical and scientific products. In most cases, you don't set out to buy the cheapest television, automobile, production equipment for your factory, or pharmaceutical: you buy what you want (see Chapter 1). You may look for the best price you can find on the gigantic TV you want, but you're not comparing it cost-wise with the seven-inch black-and-white model. Same thing goes for technical and scientific products.

In this chapter, I'm going to extend the discussion even further because most people also don't buy your product based on the economic factors you think you have to push in your marketing. At this point I'll make a bold prediction: most of what you think about how important economics is in the buying decision for your product is wrong. And to top it off, most of your opinions on how buyers look at economics are wrong, too.

As an opening salvo into marketing economics, let's return one more time to our telescope example. I've cited telescope manufacturers throughout this book as multiple-mistake offenders. But this is one of the brand busters telescope manufacturers did *not* make. Imagine the absurdity of trying to tie telescope purchases to economics. Think of the headlines you might see on telescope ads:

"See the rings of Saturn for less than $6.75 an hour."

"Less expensive than a motorboat . . . more cost-effective than a plasma TV."

"Think of the money you'll save on movie tickets by seeing the stars . . . through your new telescope!"

You get the idea. While the price of a given telescope—or telescopes in general—may have some influence on your buying decision, other economic factors have no bearing whatsoever on your purchase. You don't care about ROI. You're not worried about saving money on other activities. You want what a telescope can give you—which is, in the end, not just a clear look at stars and planets, but a sense of wonder and connection with the universe.

So why do marketers have such a love affair with ROI and other economic factors? Is buying a telescope really so much different from buying a CNC lathe, notebook computer, or a business insurance policy?

The ROI Myth

ROI (return on investment) may not be the buzzword of the moment, but it's way up there. You can find lots of other variations that relate to economics: return on assets, return on equity, gross profit, net return, revenue, and many more. They all point to what you get (economically speaking) out of the money or time or effort you put in.

I'm not completely dismissing these concepts. They're all fine metrics—good things to measure and good numbers to know. But on their own, each is just one data point and only one small component of a thoughtful marketing message.

The trouble is, lots of marketers start with ROI, and there they stay. Many business-to-business marketers treat ROI or profit (or whatever) as if it were the Promised Land. "Buy our (supply chain software/lab analyzer/GPS tracking system/your product here), and you're on your way to improved ROI!" seems to be the most prominent marketing claim for technical and scientific products. It's been that way for years, and will probably be that way for decades more.

For smart marketers who stay away from this "me too" drivel, overuse of this claim may be a good thing. It means your message has a chance to stand out in the crowd.

You see, *economics is not now, and never will be, a key differentiator.* "Economics" is a table stake—a bare minimum attribute you must have to be in the game. And listen up: you don't differentiate on bare minimums.

Somewhere in the marketing wilderness, I hear a protest: "But my product really does have a great ROI. Are you telling me I should bury that benefit?" OK, I'll play along. For the sake of argument, let's say your technical whiz-bang really does have a superior ROI—maybe even *the* superior ROI.

The product with superior ROI probably delivers it because of something it *does*. What a product does for someone, by the way, is a benefit. And people want benefits. People buy stuff based on benefits (re-read Chapter 1 if this surprises you). ROI (or profit or any other number-based fact) is a feature. In nearly all cases, people don't buy "features"; they buy what those features do. So when you make your main marketing pitch ROI, you're selling based on a feature and a pretty flimsy feature at that. Everybody knows you calculate ROI using a few hard numbers and a pile of assumptions (guesses of some sort or another). That's why I sometimes refer to it as Return on *Illusion*.

So, if I had the product with the superior ROI, instead of focusing on the economics, I'd focus my marketing on what the product does and the problems it solves. Does it speed up a process? Show them how yours does it in a way that no other product can. Does it reduce mistakes and re-work? Tell them how. And teach them how to run a trial to see it for themselves. Does it require less manpower to operate, thus reducing headcount or the headaches of hiring and training? That's a benefit you can and should talk to your audience about. So do it. Does it require less initial cash outlay, reducing the hassle of trying to get the credit limit increased? See how this works?

Here's a dirty little secret. Despite protests to the contrary, lots of people in your market don't really care about money. They care about things like running lab experiments or ending a petty disagreement among their staff. Or discovering the next big thing in their industry. Or getting home an hour early to see their kid's ball game.

The money they save, or the net return, isn't what trips their trigger. In fact, unless it's a very small business, the money *isn't even their money*. It's the company's money. But the pain or problem your product alleviates is theirs completely. The economic hoop they make a seller jump through is just an exercise so they can show the boss they weren't being stupid with the company's money.

Let's face it, no one is marketing products (and no one's buying products) with the expectation of getting a lousy ROI. Every marketer of a technical or scientific product knows how to make his ROI look good. Buyers know this. And so, they're uniformly skeptical of ROI claims made by marketers. Blowing off the marketer's ROI claims has become second nature to most buyers. Furthermore, most buyers and companies have their own methods of figuring out whether a product makes economic sense or not. They rarely cede to the marketer's method.

Marketing your product based on improved ROI, then, is like marketing puppies with heads. Of course, puppies have heads. Nothing distinctive there. So why are we even discussing it?

Some other factor—ease of use, dependability, performance, or innovation, or even profit, for example—will trump ROI and actually lead to a sale. So if you're stopping the marketing message at ROI, you've ground to a halt before you've even gotten started.

Here's another beef I have with the whole ROI thing. Most people have no clue what the term actually means. And so they use it incorrectly and look silly in the process.

Most people think ROI is money. It isn't. ROI is a ratio—in other words, a number, followed by a colon (or the word "to"), followed by another number (example: 3:1 or 3 to 1).

I recently took part in a marketing planning session with a large global marketer. Eighteen very smart people in a room for two days, including many with advanced degrees. We spent several hours on the economics surrounding the marketing strategy. As I expected, the discussion gravitated to ROI. But then something happened I didn't expect. It became clear that only one person in the room knew the real meaning and definition of the term ROI and was able to use it correctly. It was me—the guy with no advanced degrees—and with no advanced education whatsoever in accounting, finance, or economics. I shared with these smart folks the key concepts you're reading in this chapter. And to their credit they listened and learned. Now they're much better equipped to deal with the marketing side of economics. By the way, the group came to consensus. They decided to include an ROI message in their marketing but to make it a minor point. Bravo.

Back to the term ROI. When used correctly, it expresses the magnitude of return resulting from an expenditure or investment. For example, the ROI on money in a simple savings account after one year is around 1.05:1, which means you made 5 percent on your money. Financial novices (often marketers) commonly and mistakenly use ROI when they instead mean return, as in: "The ROI on that was $16,500." Using the right term for this, I would say "My *return* on that was $16,500. And that's even a little confusing, since I would need to explain whether that is gross return (before subtracting out costs) or net return (after subtracting costs). One final bash on ROI: since it's not money, you can't spend it. I can spend $16,500. But I can't spend three followed by a colon, followed by one. That's why it's often hard for buyers to get emotional and feel good about an ROI.

"Nobody Ever Got Fired for Specifying a Xerox Copier"

This headline, from before my time, is a marketing classic. In one way, it's akin to saying, "Play it safe: the gray suit will never go out of style." On the other hand, it's a skillful indictment of the "we must sell on economics" myth. It says you can buy a cheaper copier, but you probably can't trust them. ROI or economic return, after all, requires the product you purchase (and your predictions for the future) to actually work the way you say they will.

So, people do buy the more expensive copier or extruder or swappable hard drive. Even though, all things being equal, it may take longer to break even or show an ROI with the expensive purchase.

Marketing Your Brand: It's *Not* a Numbers Game

Perhaps now's a good time to examine how most businesses look at purchases and economics. The first thing to understand is that businesses look at most purchases from the standpoint of *category* reasonableness. In other words, before looking at your brand (or any other), they often ask the question, "Does this *type* of purchase seem reasonable?"

Should we buy a building? Or not? Does it make sense to lease a printing press? Or do we continue using the ones we already have? Should we make the leap into RFLP testing now, or continue using the old technology? Should we lay out funds to acquire the intellectual capital for that new software product? Or can we build it ourselves with the resources we have on hand? These are the types of initial questions buyers often ask when they get started. In essence, they're asking: "Should we do nothing or should we do something?" Should we live with things the way they are, which may be painful, economically and in other ways? Or put up with the pain of change?

This question must be answered before brand ever enters the discussion. That's why I believe you should forget about your brand at this point in an economic discussion.

Successful economic arguments almost always start with building the case for a category, not a specific brand. Before they're ready to go to the big boss, buyers first need to justify spending any money at all to solve the problem. If they can't do that, your brand (along with everybody else's) doesn't have a chance.

So, first help your audience see why it makes sense to spend some money to solve their problem. Once you've done that, your next goal should be to build preference for your brand.

Purchases based solely on economics (and thus, price) don't happen very often, but I'll admit they do sometimes. And here's how those situations shake out: the lowest price wins.

Evidence for this is very strong:

The lowest priced product rarely commands the market leader positions, even in pure commodity categories like water.

If decisions always came down to economics, pricing of every product within a category would be identical or nearly identical. You wouldn't see the wide variations in price from high to low, because category reasonableness analysis would drive the high-priced products out of business.

"But," you say, "economics don't come down to just price. ROI is partly a factor of price, but it also encompasses performance, dependability, and other factors. That's *why* no one ever got fired for buying a Xerox copier: even though it's more expensive, ROI is actually superior."

Yes, but in most cases, the expensive widget buyer is not really concerned with economics. A buyer concerned purely with economics buys the lowest-priced gizmo because low price is the only absolute in the analysis. Results, returns, or ROI must be based on assumptions or predictions of the future. Some people are quite comfortable making decisions based on predictions of the future. But economic buyers aren't.

You may think the expensive copier will work without a hitch for ten years, but you really don't know; every copier maker occasionally builds a lemon. And people concerned solely with economics don't make decisions based on assumptions. They buy based on the only number in the economic equation that isn't an assumption—the hard cost of buying your stuff. And as you'll remember from our discussion in Chapter 6, low cost is not a game we, as marketers, want to play.

So yes, there may be an economic hurdle to clear. But it probably has nothing to do with your brand. Ultimately the brand that gives the customers what they want ends up the winner. And in most cases, that "want" is way beyond money and way beyond the numbers.

What Do the People with the Money Say?

But don't take my word for it. Audiences in all sorts of markets for technical and scientific products will tell you they don't make decisions on an economic basis.

For example, a study by Purdue University surveyed the top agricultural producers in the nation.[1] These are shrewd, highly educated, successful businesspeople who use the latest technology and techniques to grow food profitably. Keep in mind that, for the most part, these business people produce undifferentiated, unbranded commodities: milk, grain, meat, cotton, eggs, and so on. The survey revealed the number-one goal of this group was not to reduce costs or even to make more money: it was to have more free time. Yet the majority of marketing "arguments" made to these people focus on economics. Hmmmmmm.

Here's another example. While researching this book, I interviewed someone who had been a senior financial executive at a large U.S. bank. This person, who happened to be a CPA, was often charged with reviewing large expenditure requests and offering his "go/no go" opinions to the bank's executive committee. Many of the purchases he and the bank considered were in the millions of dollars. Here's what he said about ROI as it relates to purchase decisions:

"Most ROI calculations are based purely on assumptions, especially in the revenue or cost-savings side of the equation, for the express purpose of justifying spending the money."

In other words, he confirmed what I've been saying: ROI is an assumption used to justify spending, not to choose a brand. It's not based on fact, and it's not really a competitive advantage for you.

I assumed then, that if he understood this, he didn't require ROI analysis for a large purchase. He practically laughed at me.

"I *always* demand an ROI—often as a way to bury the idea." he said. "I love seeing non-finance people try and make the sale on a financial basis. I blow them away every time.

"It's the *non*-financial arguments I have trouble picking apart. They're always driven by emotions, and I have no idea how to expose the flaws in emotional calculations."

How interesting. At least in this top financial executive's opinion, focusing on ROI is the way to **bury** the project. If you can't make the numbers look right, the financial guy will kill the expenditure—and, p.s., he knows the assumptions you used to build your economic case are all smoke and mirrors.

But give him an emotional argument, and he doesn't quite know what to do. Instead of telling him how many copies per minute the new machine will make, tell him his assistant is going to quit if he has to deal with that old copier one more day. And tell him that low turnover is the benchmark indicator that correlates most closely with market share in your sector (assuming that's true).

Of course, you may think this is a one-in-a-million kind of CFO who knows how to use ROI to squash your plans. Not hardly. Most financial people are cut from the same cloth. They know how to manipulate economic arguments to avoid spending. It's their job. And they love it.

Here's a final bit of advice from this seasoned CFO. Make your economic case based on *reasonableness*. Forget promises like ROI and return. Those get etched into the CFO's brain under the heading of "guarantee." And believe me, when your prediction of future return or ROI doesn't come true, he'll be the first to whip out the "guarantee" paperwork or slides you left with him and slap a fraud action on you via your boss. The guy wants his money, and you said . . .

So how do you make an economic reasonableness argument without making claims about ROI or return? First, understand the language of finance and financial decisions. My advice is to focus on breakeven. In other words, explain to your audience how much of an improvement is required to pay back the cost of your product or service. Be conservative in your numbers. Make the numbers a little lower or worse than they might normally expect. If they think you've shorted yourself, they'll let you know, which means they're arguing your case for you. And that's a good thing. (By the way, you can use breakeven analysis with your boss, when it comes to supporting a marketing budget or expense.)

Here's how to do a breakeven analysis.

First, find out what the key economic metrics are in your market. If you're selling laboratory equipment to hospitals that run hundreds of blood tests a day, maybe the metric is labor cost per test or tests per hour (or some other measure). If your market uses several, show several. (Then include data for all the measures in your marketing materials: brochures, website, and presentations.) To the extent you can, show your audience it's reasonable to expect they'll get their money back. If you can't, be truthful about that as well. Maybe they'll tell you they aren't really making the decision based on the numbers, after all.

"Nobody Ever Got Promoted for Making Plan"

A senior marketing executive with a large and growing multinational company said that to me a few years back. In a sort of backhanded way, Stan (not his real name) told me hitting a budget or controlling expenses never paves the way to a promotion. So when you reduce your marketing arguments to economics you end up appealing to people who by and large aren't superstars. Is that the position you want for your brand?

Here's the point where most people want to disagree with me. Is this what you're thinking? "You don't get it, Chris. Everybody in the _____ industry (fill in the blank here—any industry will do) focuses on economics. We've got to play the game. Plus, our ROI's better." Spare me. It's going to be awfully hard for you to distinguish your brand if you do the same thing as everybody else.

Don't be confused. Am I telling you not to have an economic worksheet your sales folks can walk a customer through or a cost savings calculator feature on your website? No. Am I telling you to clear the economic hurdle and then get back to the pain? You bet I am. That's the marketing high ground where you can differentiate the brand and win the business. Seriously, how distinctive is your brand when it's reduced to a few numbers on a spreadsheet? Not very.

Believing you must sell your product on an economic basis is a mistake you can easily avoid.

Avoiding Brand Buster #7 = Economics 101 + Smart Marketing

Avoiding this mistake is simple: address the economics when you have to, then quickly move to the aspects of your product that truly address the customer's pain or problem. I realize this isn't easy. After all, it requires an intimate understanding of what your audience really wants, not just the ability to run a spreadsheet. It requires you to address your buyers at their point of pain; remember, most marketers are too busy falling in love with their product to really look through the buyer's eyes. And it requires focus—knowing very well what problems your product can solve, and what problems it can't.

So here's the fix for this, our last mistake. I call it: The 3 Rules of Marketing Economics . . .

1. Economic analysis = category reasonableness

2. If the buyer's pain is economic, the buyer seeks to cut expenses—and will buy the cheapest product.

3. Clear the economic hurdle; then get back to the pain.

It takes a smart marketer to avoid the trap of selling on an economic basis. And now that you've made it through the last of the brand busters, you're probably feeling a bit smarter. But you'd probably feel positively brilliant if you had a little more advice about avoiding marketing mistakes, yes?

Good. Because that's where we're going next.

What Should You Remember from Reading this Chapter?

☞ **Economics is not** now, and never will be, **a key differentiator.** "Economics" is a table stake—a bare minimum attribute you must have to be in the game.

☞ **Some other factor**—ease of use, dependability, performance, innovation, or even profit—**will trump ROI and actually lead to a sale.**

☞ **Successful economic arguments almost always start with building the case for a category,** not a specific brand.

☞ **Ultimately, the brand that gives the customers what they want ends up the winner.** And in most cases, that "want" is way beyond money and way beyond the numbers.

☞ **ROI is an assumption used to justify spending,** not to choose a brand.

☞ Make your economic case based on reasonableness. **Forget promises like ROI and return.**

☞ **Reasonableness focuses on breakeven.** Explain to your market how much of an improvement is required to pay back the cost of your product or service.

☞ **Address the economics when you have to,** then quickly move to other aspects of your product that truly address the customer's pain or problem.

The Smart Stuff: How to Avoid the Seven Common Mistakes

WHEW! YOU'VE MADE IT. Not that I think it's been such a tough slog to get here. But if you've gotten this far, I'm guessing you've been pretty honest with yourself. You've probably recognized your actions—or, at least, your company's actions—in a few of the mistakes. Although I've spent some time throughout this book offering advice on how you can avoid making these mistakes and what you could be doing differently in each instance, before we close, it seems as if a bit of review and some general advice might be in order.

So, what have we learned up to this point?

First, we learned that most marketers get hung up addressing customer "needs" when they should really be addressing "wants." People don't really buy what they need. That's because needs are based more on rationality (features) and wants are based more on emotion (benefits), and all great marketing appeals first to emotion.

Next, we learned that marketers, especially marketers of technical and scientific products, tend to fall in love with their technology. It's really a matter of getting hung up on product features and ignoring your customer. Go ahead and love your product; just don't expect your customer to care the way you do. And please, stop imagining that your product or your market is somehow the only one that requires you to talk to your customers as if they were robots.

Third, marketing is truly part art, part science—and fully neither.

Use research to help you understand your customers and shape your messages, but don't fall victim to analysis paralysis. Let your creativity flow, but make sure your ideas have a basis in reality.

Fourth, most marketers really want to please everyone, and it's *always* a mistake. You can't really be big but small. You can't really be round but square. Remember that great brands are, in most of their attributes, D students. You have to find the continent, territory, or island you can command and stake your claim boldly.

Remember that people forget. Remember that people forget. Frequency helps your customers remember your message. And awareness, all by itself, helps build brand preference. Remember that people forget.

Do you think the problem with your sales is that the price of your product is too high? It's probably not. High price sometimes becomes the excuse salespeople use to justify mediocre performance. And cutting price can have a dramatic effect on your bottom line; you will probably have to sell many more units to maintain the same level of profitability. Cut price as a last resort, but be sure you first do your homework. Know for sure that high price does indeed stand in the way of sales before you start slashing.

Finally, remember that economic appeals really aren't what sell most products. Buyers understand they need their purchases to provide a certain level of value. Delivering dollar value is merely a table stake. The winning product must appeal to the buyer on a different level as well. Address economics, but move past them quickly to the customer's real point of pain.

When you remember these points, you're miles ahead in making and executing a great marketing plan. But I've also got three more rules to keep in mind that transcend all the common mistakes we talked about.

Seven Common Mistakes Bite The Dust:
Three Classic Rules of Great Marketing

Remember the best-selling book by Robert Fulghum, *All I Really*

Need To Know I Learned In Kindergarten? Sometimes I think all I *really* need to know about marketing can be summed up in three simple points. (I can hear the catcalls already: "*Now* he tells us. We waded through this entire book only to find out we only needed to read the last chapter." Well, not exactly. It's usually good to have a handle on what you're doing wrong before you can make it right. Plus, traipsing through the Brand Busters was kind of fun, wasn't it?) Here they are:

Classic Rule #1: People Forget.

Yes, I devoted a whole chapter to this one. Yes, I've said it over and over again. But it's true: people forget just about everything. They forget the anniversaries of the most important events in their lives: weddings, birthdays, and historical events. They forget things that, at the time, seemed big and important. For example, who won the Super Bowl four years ago? Who was the losing vice presidential candidate in the last election? Why exactly did that project drive you crazy last month (the one you slaved over for so many hours)? What was the name of the protagonist in that novel you couldn't put down last week?

When people forget even the most important things in their lives, you sure as heck can't expect them to remember your marketing pitch. You have to be in their minds when they're ready to buy, which means you don't want to give your prospects the opportunity to forget about you. Think frequency. Think recency.

Every product is different and every market is different. The decision to buy ink cartridges really isn't the same as the decision to buy a radar system. But you can never take for granted that your prospects remember you. If you've been off their radar screens for any time at all, they don't.

Classic Rule #2: Me First.

I'm no psychologist—although I think you have to know a little bit about human behavior to be a successful marketer. And what I've observed again and again over the last couple of decades in business is that people are concerned about themselves before they're concerned about anything else.

This is not to suggest that people aren't altruistic or that they don't make sacrifices for others. People certainly do put in long hours working for their churches and charities and friends and neighbors and ne'er-do-well nephews. And people work hard for their employers—or, if they're the employers, for the good of their employees. I'm not disputing or minimizing the good work lots of people do.

But there's a component of selfishness even in the most selfless work. Let's face it: if you give a hunk of money to your favorite charity, part of the reason you do so is the way it makes you feel for having done it. If you volunteer to sell cookies at the high school swim team fundraiser, it's probably because they really do need those new warm-up suits (and because your daughter is on the swim team).

What does this mean to you as a marketer? It means, as I've been saying throughout this book, that you have to make personal appeals to your audience, and you have to keep their actual desires in mind. Your customers may seem to want greater productivity, but what they actually want is for their jobs to be less frustrating. They may seem to want 1366 x 768 and a 5,000 to 1 contrast ratio, but what they really want is to see the football game larger than life in the comfort of their own homes.

Remember the themes I've returned to time and again in this book: it's not about the technology. It's not about the money. It's not about the features. If I'm the buyer, it's all about *me*.

Classic Rule #3: Emotion Rules.

If there's one thing you take away from this book, perhaps this should be it. People do not respond to marketing messages with their heads. To use the above example, I don't even know what a "contrast ratio" is. I just know that when I'm watching the game at home, I want to feel like I'm actually on the field. You can throw specs at me all day long, and I don't care. I don't care about telescopes: I want to see the stars. I don't care about horsepower: I want to go fast. Do your marketing a favor. Fill in the blanks: "I don't care about _____. I want _____."

This is not to say that the head has no place in people's buying decisions. The closer you get to making the sale, the more the details matter. If you're trying to decide between two cars you like, you're going to take lots of factors into consideration, including price, performance, repair record, and resale value.

But remember two things. First, this is a book about marketing, not about sales. And the goal of marketing, more often than not (and certainly initially), is awareness and consideration. When it's time for you to buy a car, I want you to be thinking about me. That's marketing's job. Getting your name on the contract is a job for the sales department. Because it's not my area of expertise, I'll stop short of saying emotion rules when it comes to sales; in fact, I'll suggest that, in many cases, you have to handle the details in a convincing way to pay off the emotional appeal of marketing with the more cerebral points that allow your prospects to justify their gut instincts. Again, to use cars as the example, I'm not saying you ignore horsepower and gas mileage and trunk size and headroom. I'm saying you would do well to remember that nobody's going to be interested in your car initially for the practical reasons that are best left to your salespeople, not your advertising.

I'm also saying that, if those are the features you really need to sell, you need to connect them with your prospects emotionally. Few people really care about horsepower, although a lot of people care about going fast. Nobody cares about trunk dimensions, although a lot of people care about whether they can fit three suitcases and their golf clubs back there so they can travel more comfortably. Even when you're talking features, you need to think about what people really want and communicate with them in emotional terms.

And the second point is, even at the sales level, we really do buy what we like and want. If your choice of automobiles comes down to one that's a little flashier versus one that's a little more practical, you're ultimately going to base your decision on who you perceive yourself to be—or how you want to be perceived. Are you a little flashier or a little more practical yourself? What do people expect of you? What do you want them to think? Don't kid yourself into thinking that emotion plays no role in technical and scientific purchases. Logic may have a seat at the table, but emotion *rules*.

How to Become a Really Good Marketer in About a Minute

Over the years, all sorts of gurus have invested years of time and energy and shared literally millions of words of advice about marketing. If you've made it this far, you've absorbed lots of my words. I stand by them. They've served me and my clients well for decades.

I know I've provided a lot to think about here. I've listed seven common mistakes. I've told you how to beat them. Heck, I just offered a list of three classic rules of great marketing. Yet, I feel compelled to simplify the message even further. What do you really, truly have to remember above all else when you're creating an effective marketing plan? I think it's this:

Remember you're not talking to data points. You're talking to people.

That's it. You're talking to people, and people don't want to be forgotten. Or talked down to. Or made to look silly. So, you need to show people you understand and care about them. You need to show up at the places they hang around. You need to say things they care about. And you don't have the luxury of wasting their time. Don't lie to them. Don't bore them. Don't try to interest them in things they don't want. Don't talk to them about focal length when they really want to see the moon. Communicate succinctly. Tell them *one thing*. Tell them convincingly. Respect their time and intelligence.

And for goodness' sake, remember people are emotional beings. They're not dots on a line graph. Nobody respects market research more than I do. But there's an ancient Zen precept that says, "A finger pointing at the moon is not the moon." Research is the finger. Real people are the moon.

And that's it: a one-minute lesson in marketing excellence. Remember above all else to respect your audience as people, and you'll survive even the deadliest of marketing mistakes.

More Mistakes?

Finally, I hope you've enjoyed reading this book as much as I've enjoyed writing it. It's been fun for me to share what I know about marketing. I hope it's been useful to you as well. The world needs better marketing; goodness knows, a lot of it isn't very good. I'm reminded of what's known as Sturgeon's Law, named for the late science fiction author Theodore Sturgeon. Once when he'd gotten tired of "serious" literary types pointing out that most science fiction wasn't very good, he said, "Sure, 90 percent of science fiction is crap. That's because 90 percent of everything is crap."

Too true. Most marketing is crap, because most marketers fall victim to at least one of the Seven Mistakes. I don't believe that's going to change anytime soon.

Some may wonder why a marketing guy like me would write this kind of a book. Am I not afraid that I'm giving away trade secrets? That now my competitors know exactly how I work so they can use my methods against me? That *you* might be one of those competitors, and that now I'd better watch my back?

Not really. There's plenty of space out there for excellent marketing and heady competition. Because I know that most marketing is crap.

(I also know that people—including you—forget. So even though you've now gotten to the end of this book, I'm going to suggest that, from time to time, you pick it up and at least skim it again. You'll be surprised by all the good stuff you've forgotten. I practically guarantee it.)

All the more reason for you to take these lessons to heart and strive to do great marketing. You'll stand out all the more, and your company will be more successful. Maybe you'll finally be able to purchase that tropical island you've been dreaming about and spend the rest of your days sipping mango daiquiris on the beach.

And frankly, I'd love to hear from you. Please feel free to visit *www.5metacom.com/BrandBusters/htm*—or drop me a note at *cwirthwein@5metacom.com* to share your stories about common marketing mistakes and challenges from the world of technical and scientific products. Maybe you've run into a whole new class of mistake that I haven't touched. Maybe you have some rules of your own you'd like to bandy about.

Or maybe you just want to tell me how wonderful I am and how my book has changed your life forever.

Hey, I'm not immune to emotional appeals. Me first. Remember?

References

Chapter 1

1 Ogilvy, D. *Ogilvy on Advertising.* Crown, 1983.

2 Maslow, A. A Theory of Human Motivation. *Psychological Review,* 50, 1943.

3 Loechner, J. "Want Beats Need for Over 1/3 of New Car Buyers." Center for Media Research. Available at *www.centerformediaresearch.com* as of May 16, 2005.

Chapter 2

1 Moore, G. *Crossing the Chasm: Marketing and Selling High-tech Products to Mainstream Consumers.* HarperBusiness, 1991.

2 Reeves, R. *Reality in Advertising.* Knopf, 1961.

3 Pirsig, R. *Zen and the Art of Motorcycle Maintenance.* Morrow, 1974.

4 Copy Chasers. *Business Marketing,* June 1999.

Chapter 3

1 Reeves, R. *Reality in Advertising.* Knopf, 1961.

2 Hauser, J. and Griffin, A. "The Voice of the Customer." *Marketing Science,* Vol.12, No. 1, Winter 1993.

3 Hopkins, C. *Scientific Advertising.* 1923; with intro by David Ogilvy, Crown, 1966.

4 Peters, R. and Wedel, M. "Attention Capture and Transfer in Advertising: Brand, Pictorial, and Text-size Effects." *Journal of Marketing,* April 2004.

5 Von Keitz. Symposium for Communications Research, Saarbrucken, 1985.

6 DuPlessis, E. *The Advertised Mind.* Kogan Page, 2005.

7 Hermie, P., Lanckriet, T., Lansloot, K. and Peeters, S. *Stop|Watch.* Media-logue, 2005.

Chapter 4

1 Hawkins, S.A. and Hoch, S.J. Low-Involvement Learning: Memory Without Evaluation. *Journal of Consumer Research,* September 1992.

2 Shapiro, S., MacInnis, D. and Heckler, S. "The Effects of Incidental Ad

Exposure on the Formation of Consideration Sets." *Journal of Consumer Research*, Vol. 24, June 1997.

3 Latzman, A. "IT Marketing Guide: 2004 Data for Software, Hardware, and Services Marketers." *MarketingSherpa: Practical Know-How & Case Studies*, May 2004.

Chapter 5

1 *Sky & Telescope,* "New Track Media." Vol. 103, No. 5, May 2002.

2 Ebbinghaus, H. in *Advertising Reach and Frequency* by C. McDonald, NTC Business Books, 1995.

3 Reber, R., Winkielman, P. and Schwarz, N. "Effects of Perceptual Fluency on Affective Judgments." *Psychological Science.* January 1998.

4 Kunst-Wilson, W., Jajonc, R. "Affective Discrimination of Stimuli that Cannot be Recognized." *Science.* 1980; 207:557-558.

5 Kiljewski, V. and Yoon, E. Penn State Institute for the Study of Business Markets, 1990.

6 Rogers, E. *Diffusion of Innovations*. The Free Press, 1962.

7 Murry, G. and Jenkins, R. "The Concept of Effective Reach in Advertising." *Journal of Advertising Research*, May/June 1992.

8 McDonald, C. *Advertising Reach and Frequency: Maximizing Advertising Results Through Effective Frequency*. McGraw-Hill, 2nd edition, 1996.

9 Jones, J. *When Ads Work: New Proof That Advertising Triggers Sales*. M.E. Sharpe, Inc., October 2006.

10 Ephron, E. "Media Planning: Recency Planning." *Admap*, February 1997.

Chapter 6

1 Rao, A., Bergen, M., and Davis, S. "How to Fight a Price War." *Harvard Business Review on Marketing,* Harvard Business School Press, 2001.

2 Geisman, J., and Maruskin, J. "Pricing Strategy a Case for Discount Discipline." *Harvard Business Review,* Nov. 2006; 84(11):30.

3 van Westendorp, P. "NSS – Price Sensitivity Meter: A New Approach to Study Consumer Perception of Price." *Proc. ESOMAR Congress*, 1976.

4 Marder, E. *The Laws of Choice: Predicting Customer Behavior*. Free Press, 1997.

Chapter 7

1 *1998 Commercial Producer Survey,* Purdue University, Center for Food and Agricultural Business, 1998.

Index

About the Author

CHRIS WIRTHWEIN is one of our country's most accomplished marketing professionals. As CEO of the advertising agency 5MetaCom, Chris has worked with many of the world's leading companies in medical devices, financial services, pharmaceuticals, agribusiness, and scores of other industries. His client list reads like a "Who's Who" of successful technical and scientific brands and has included Eli Lilly and Company, Dow AgroSciences, Bristol-Myers, Land O'Lakes, Elanco Animal Health, Roche Diagnostics, Black & Decker, Honeywell, and many others.

Chris is a 1979 graduate of Butler University in Indianapolis, Indiana, with a Bachelor of Arts in journalism. He began his advertising career as a copywriter and account executive in 1980. Since that time he has developed hundreds of successful campaigns and strategic plans for regional, national, and international business-to-business clients. He has also taught at the university level, having served as a guest lecturer at the Purdue University Center for Agricultural Business and at Butler University, in Advertising Principles and Practice.

Today Chris is a frequent speaker at marketing forums and professional and trade events and has appeared on television numerous times as a commentator on marketing and advertising topics.

He is a member of the American Advertising Association, Indiana Federation of Advertising Agencies, a past board member and marketing committee chair of the Indiana 4-H Foundation, and past president of the National Agri-Marketing Association, Mid-America Chapter, and a former member of the Professional Pricing Society.